PETER PUCK'S
Greatest Moments in
HOCKEY

with Brian McFarlane

THE LIBRARY SHOPPE

Credits

I'd like to thank my teammates for helping me with this book. Fast-fingered writers like Elizabeth Boyd and Doug Lowe. Flashy photographers like Robert Shaver and Steve Babineau who took many of the exciting action photos.

Other photo credits go to: AP Laserphoto, pp. 6, 7; Canadian Press, p.15; Jac Holland, p.25; Jim Lipa, p.26; Federal Archives, pp. 16, 17, 19, 30, 36, 50, 51, 61, 62, 81, 86, 87; Turofsky Collection, pp. 34, 36, 76; American Airlines, p. 57.

Special thanks to artist Bill Reid, the man with the magic brush.

This book is for Brenda because
I've always felt very close to her.

Text © Copyright 1980 Brian McFarlane Enterprises Ltd.
Peter Puck © Copyright 1980 Hanna-Barbera Productions, Inc.

Canadian Cataloguing in Publication Data

McFarlane, Brian, 1931-
    Peter Puck's greatest moments in hockey

ISBN 0-919161-02-2

1. Hockey - History - Juvenile literature.
I. Title.

GV846.5.M32   j796.96'2   C80-094688-X

Printed in Canada by RBW Inc.

Contents

Introduction

I'm the world's most famous hockey puck and I've been a part of the game's most dramatic moments. I've been zapped into nets all over the world by hockey's biggest stars. I've been doused with champagne and dropped in the Stanley Cup by playoff winners in the NHL. I'll never forget Moscow in '72 when Paul Henderson slipped me over the goal line with 34 seconds to play, ending the "series of the century." In 1980, like countless millions, I marveled at the way the young Americans rose up and grabbed the gold at Lake Placid, after everybody said the Russians were a shoo-in for the Olympic medals.

I've ridden the sticks of modern day stars like Phil Esposito, Bobby Orr, Guy Lafleur and Wayne Gretzky right into the record book and I'll never forget the brilliance of yesterday's heroes, men with colorful names like "Cyclone" Taylor, "Rocket" Richard and "Terrible" Ted Lindsay.

Fans often ask, "Peter, how do you manage to play in so many games in so many cities, year after year? Yet you never wear out and you never get tired. How come?" I just laugh and say, "That's *my* secret. But it helps if you love your job."

It's no secret I love being a hockey star. I'm proud to be called the imp of the ice. And I enjoy keeping a record of the game's greatest moments.

I hope you enjoy reading about some of these moments in the pages ahead.

Best of luck,

Peter was so proud to be part of the drama at Lake Placid.

1 The Miracle on Main Street

As the star of the world's fastest team sport, I get to visit many of the world's greatest cities—New York, Los Angeles, Montreal—even Moscow. But one of my greatest moments in hockey took place in a little town high in the mountains of northern New York state in February, 1980. You guessed it—the town was Lake Placid.

I could hardly believe my luck when I found out I was going to be part of the big

hockey tournament in Lake Placid. It was an Olympic hockey tournament and somehow, international hockey always seems to bring out the best in players and teams.

But no one could have predicted that the 1980 Winter Games would produce one of the greatest upsets in hockey history, a triumph so incredible that all of North America got caught up in it. At the finish, they called it the Miracle on Main Street.

1

During most of the Olympic competition, Main Street in Lake Placid buzzed with talk about the accomplishments of speed skater Eric Heiden. This former hockey player from Minnesota collected gold medals, five of them, like some fellows collect hockey pucks. I'm glad he didn't challenge me to a race. I'm pretty fast but I'd never be able to keep pace with Eric.

Then suddenly, all the attention turned from Eric to the U.S. hockey team. After a 2-2 tie against Sweden in the opening game, the young Americans scored a major upset over Czechoslovakia by 7-3.

After that, the Olympic schedule gave the U.S. squad three fairly easy games against Norway, Rumania and West Germany before matching them against the Soviet Union in the first game of a two-game championship round.

The young Americans skated over Norway, Rumania and West Germany before the big game with the Soviet Union.

2

I recall asking Mike Eruzione, the U.S. captain, about the Soviets before the tournament and he said, "Pete, they're the best. They've won every gold medal at the Olympics for the past twenty years. If we're ever going to beat them, this is the time and the place to do it."

The game was played on Friday, February 22 and it turned out to be one of the most thrilling games I've ever been in. What a shame the action wasn't carried live on U.S. television. ABC Sports, which had paid $15.5 million for TV rights to the Games, asked the Olympic Organizing Committee to switch the U.S.-Soviet game, scheduled for 5 p.m., with the Sweden-Finland game, scheduled for 8:30 p.m., so that everyone could see the game on television. Someone on the Olympic Organizing Committee talked with someone from the U.S. Ice Hockey Association. Then someone from the International Ice Hockey Federation pointed out that the games could not be switched without permission of all four clubs involved in the final round. Apparently, the Soviet team vetoed the switch because they wanted an earlier start. But the American public was deprived of seeing a rare moment in Olympic history.

U.S. coach Herb Brooks gave his young players an inspirational pep talk before the game. "You were born to be hockey players," said Brooks. "You were meant to be here. This moment is yours. So let's have poise and possession of the puck."

The poise of the Americans was shaken in the first period when Vladimir Krutov tipped a shot behind goaltender Jim Craig.

The U.S. tied the score five minutes later when Buzz Schneider whipped a forty-foot shot past the glove of Soviet goaltender Tretiak.

The Soviets stormed back and took a 2-1 lead when Sergei Makarov took a pass in the slot and slammed a twenty-footer past Craig.

With time running out in the period, the Soviets became careless. Dave Silk carried the puck up the ice and lobbed it at Tretiak with just a few seconds to play. Tretiak let it bounce well out in front of him. That's when Mark Johnston jumped through the Soviet defense, grabbed the puck on his stick and slipped it in behind Tretiak. The goal came with just one second to play.

That was the end for Tretiak. "Tretiak has not played well in this competition and he is not playing well tonight," said Soviet coach Victor Yurzinov. He replaced the Soviet Union's most famous netminder with blond Vladimir Myshkin.

Myshkin had an easy time of it in the second period with only two shots to handle. At the other end of the rink, Jim Craig was sensational, stopping all but one of a dozen shots. Alexander Maltsev slipped through to beat Craig cleanly. That goal gave the Soviets a 3-2 lead.

In the third period, the stubborn Soviet defenders again prevented the Americans from getting even one shot on goal for the first seven minutes of play.

Then, as they had done so often in previous tournament games, the U.S. players began their comeback. Krutov of Russia took a penalty. While he was off the ice, Mark Johnston swiped at the puck with his stick and knocked it into the net. That tied the score 3-3.

Just one minute and 21 seconds later, Mike Eruzione slapped a high, hard shot over the glove of Myshkin for the go-ahead goal. There was an incredible explosion of noise. The fans stamped their feet and roared their approval. They waved their American flags. Poor Eruzione was pounded to the ice by his teammates but he didn't seem to mind. Meanwhile, the Soviet players stood and watched. At that moment they appeared to realize that the gold medal was slipping out of their grasp.

Still, they didn't quit. For the final ten minutes they stormed after the tying goal, but the pressure was on and their passes were off target. They failed to get many hard shots at Craig. They even failed to

Helmut Balderis, from the Central Red Army
Team, was a big scoring star for the Soviets.

4

Young Myshkin replaced the veteran star Tretiak in the Soviet goal.

pull their goaltender for an extra attacker in the final minute.

There was bedlam at the buzzer. Players and fans rushed at Craig and congratulated him. A combination of his superb goaltending and the unquenchable drive for victory displayed by the young Americans paid off in one of the most stunning upsets in Olympic hockey history.

Later, emerging from the showers, Craig said, "We had to prove ourselves all year, we had to prove ourselves tonight, and we'll have to prove ourselves again on Sunday. The Soviets were ripe for defeat, but they played with a lot of class. We respect them but we got what we deserved."

Soviet coach Yurzinov praised Craig's play.

"I would like to give very high marks to the American team and especially to their goaltender, who was just fantastic. Unluckily, our team made some very bad mistakes on defense."

Outside the arena, thousands of fans paraded up and down Main Street, cheering and waving and celebrating the American triumph.

"U.S.A., U.S.A., U.S.A.," they cheered.

"We're number one. We're number one." they yelled.

Yes, they were number one for the moment. But remember, there was still a major obstacle between the Americans and the gold medal. That obstacle was Finland.

The U.S. team met Finland on Sunday morning with millions of fans caught up in the excitement of it all. This game was televised and tickets for the contest were as hard to find as a dress in a dressing room.

I met one fan who hollered, "I paid $150

5

There was bedlam at the buzzer.
It was a stunning upset.

for this ticket, Pete, but I'd have gladly paid a thousand. It's been twenty years since we won a gold medal in hockey and I'm not going to miss this for anything. No sirree."

The Finns gave the Americans a battle that'll long be remembered. A smoking slapshot from inside the blue line midway through the first period eluded Jim Craig and Finland took a 1-0 lead.

But Mike Eruzione and his teammates didn't panic.

"We knew after the very first shift that they couldn't skate with us," Eruzione said later. "They just don't come up with enough offense to win by a lot of goals."

So the Americans put more pressure on the Finns and tied the game at 4:39 of the second period. Steve Christoff slid me through the legs of the Finnish goaltender, Jorma Valtonen.

But two minutes later, the Finns regained the lead when Mikko Leinonen tapped a goalmouth pass behind Craig.

And that was the setting for another American comeback, similar to the one that demolished the Soviets two days earlier.

Phil Verchota took a clever pass from Dave Christian and drilled a twenty-five footer through Valtonen's pads. That made it 2-2.

Mark Johnston then fought for the puck behind the Finnish goal and slipped a pass out to Rob McClanahan. McClanahan waited for the Finnish goalie to make his move, and when the goalie went down, the American forward slipped the puck through his legs into the net. The Americans took the lead for the first time.

That seemed to finish off the Finns with about half a period to play. But then the Americans ran into penalty problems that could have been disastrous. They took two penalties in a row but some superb penalty killing kept the Finns at bay.

6

Goalie Jim Craig, wrapped in the Stars and Stripes, was hockey's biggest hero.

Then, while playing short-handed, Mark Johnston stole the puck and moved around one defender. He saw his shot blocked by Valtonen but spotted a short rebound. He swatted the puck into the net and that was the clinching goal, the final tally in a 4-2 triumph.

Oh, how they cheered at the end of the game. What a wild celebration! It seemed to go on forever.

When the players were finally able to get to their dressing room, they were joined by U.S. Vice President Walter Mondale. President Carter called from Washington and spoke to coach Brooks and captain Mike Eruzione.

"Tell all the players on the team how much I love them," said the President, "and I look forward to seeing you all at the White House tomorrow."

Mike Eruzione summed up the feelings of most of the players.

"Six months ago we came together from different walks of life and different ethnic backgrounds," he said, "and we jelled into a team. It's been a tremendous thrill for all of us. The sad part is, after our visit to the White House, we'll all be going our separate ways. Who knows when we'll see each other again. That's a great disappointment."

Ten, twenty, fifty years from now, when players from this team come back to Lake Placid, they'll show their children and their grandchildren the hills for ski jumping, downhill and slalom, the slick runs for bobsled and luge, and finally, the hockey arena. They'll relive the thrill of their stunning upset, feel again the weight of the gold medal against the chest. They'll recall the words of Coach Brooks, "You were born to be hockey players. You were meant to be here. This moment is yours."

The moment, like the medal, was and is pure gold.

In Lake Placid, they'll never forget the Miracle on Main Street.

No team could stop the Flyers. They flattened all opponents and went week after week without losing.

2 The Flyers' Undefeated Streak

I'm glad I'm a hockey puck. I'd much rather be a hard little hockey puck than a big, fat basketball or a funny-looking football. I'm faster than those two fellows and much more difficult to control in a game.

There's one thing we all have in common. The team that controls us the most usually wins the game. The team that consistently demonstrates good puck control or ball control may win several games in a row. In sports, this is called a streak.

There have been many famous streaks in sports history.

My friend, Barry Basketball, has often bragged about a couple of streaks in his sport.

"I'll never forget a college team from UCLA," said Barry, bouncing up and down. "Would you believe they won eighty-eight straight games? I didn't think anybody would ever beat them."

"Pooh on college basketball," growled

The Flyers made quick line changes and kept the pressure on.

Freddie Football, muscling his way into the conversation. "Just a bunch of kids playing weak opponents. If you want a college streak that really means something, take Oklahoma in football. A few years ago they won forty-seven games in a row. I should know 'cause I was there."

"Pardon me, guys," I said, "But you're both talking college sports. Let's talk about the men who play for pay. Who do you think holds the longest undefeated streak in *pro* sports?"

"Beats me," said Freddie Football.

"That record belongs to hockey and the Philadelphia Flyers," I said. "Would you believe thirty-five games without a single loss?"

"That's a lot of games," admitted Barry.

"Yeah, I can't think of any pro football team ever going that long without losing," said Freddie.

I decided I'd better educate my two friends about the finer points of pro sport, so I told them all about the Flyers and their famous streak. But I started off by describing the Montreal Canadiens record that was established in 1977-78. The Canadiens went twenty-eight games without a loss. They won twenty-three and tied five before their streak was snapped by the Boston Bruins.

At the time, the fans said it would be years before another team came along to compile such a mark. They said it would take a team of real superstars to top that record. But then, just two seasons later, the Philadelphia Flyers came along—and believe me, they didn't have many superstars—and played game after game without tasting defeat.

The streak began after the Flyers lost to Atlanta 9-2 in the second game of the

9

season. The very next night they went out and beat Toronto 4-3 and that was the start of a remarkable romp around the NHL.

One day after the Flyers had gone two or three weeks without a loss, coach Pat Quinn said to me, "Pete, I never thought we'd get a start like this. As you know, we've adopted a new style this season and we don't have all the wrinkles ironed out yet. They won't be calling us the Broad Street Bullies any more. The old Flyer style, with a lot of muscle and brawling was fine for this team in its time. But hockey is different now and that style just won't work any longer. From now on, we're going to play like the Canadiens and the Soviets. There'll be players in motion at all times. We'll emphasize skating and passing and give our opponents no time to relax."

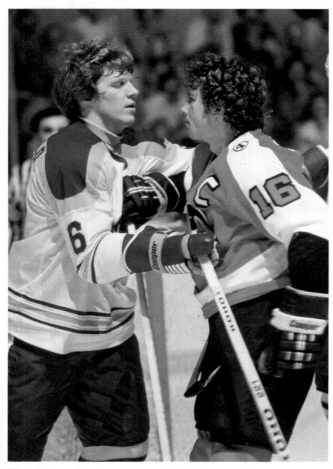

The Flyers beat a strong Buffalo team in game number 35. Schoenfeld and Clarke glare at each other.

"That's the way to talk, Pat," I told him. "I never cared much for the old Flyer style anyway. Guys like Dave Schultz were always more interested in fighting than stickhandling. Good luck to you and your new system."

Well, Quinn's system worked beautifully. As the points piled up, the Flyer penalty minutes went down. Midway through the streak they were averaging only seventeen penalty minutes per game. During their roughhouse days, they often averaged that many during the playing of the national anthem.

The Flyers were a happy, relaxed bunch throughout the streak. The two goalies, rookie Pete Peeters and veteran Phil Myre, were thrilled to be part of such a team effort. Peeters said, "I have to keep pinching myself to make sure I'm really a part of this," and Myre added, "This is the greatest accomplishment that I've been part of in my pro career. I was on a Stanley Cup team early in my career in Montreal but I really didn't play very much. Last year I played in St. Louis and we took a lot of beatings. I never dreamed I'd be a part of something like this."

The players got a little nervous after they tied the Canadiens old record of twenty-eight games without defeat. And no wonder. They faced the Boston Bruins, a tough opponent, in game number twenty-nine.

Bobby Clarke, named as assistant coach to Quinn early in the season, was relieved when the Boston game was over and the streak was still intact. "I felt a bit of tension in that game," Bobby admitted. "But we came through all right. Of course, if we don't do well in the playoffs at the end of the season this streak won't mean a thing, will it?"

I told him, "It's still a pretty big deal to most fans, Bobby. The tributes are pouring in and all the big magazines and TV networks are following the Flyers. Wouldn't it be something if the Flyers

Bill Barber played some of the finest hockey of his career throughout the Streak.

There was a comic post script to the streak, thanks to Winnipeg goalie Gary Smith.

went right through the rest of the season without losing another game?"

Of course that was an impossible goal. The Montreal Canadiens once played an entire eighty game schedule and lost only eight games, but imagine any team playing the same number of games in the NHL and losing only one game.

Early in the New Year, on January 7, the Flyers faced the young, confident Minnesota North Stars in Bloomington, Min-

nesota. The Flyers were fresh from two more victories over New York and Buffalo and the streak had reached thirty-five games. Could they make it thirty-six?

The game was strictly no contest. The North Stars zapped the puck into the Flyer net seven times while the Flyers only got one shot past the North Star goalie. The long streak was over.

At the final buzzer there was a lot of shoving and pushing by the players. It didn't seem to occur to the Flyers to congratulate the North Stars. Aside from that, the Flyers displayed a lot of class throughout their long assault on the record.

There was a humorous postscript to all of this excitement when the Flyers played their next game on home ice against the Winnipeg Jets. Now it just happens that the Winnipeg goalie, Gary Smith, was one of the most colorful characters in hockey. In the Winnipeg dressing room, Smith winked and told his teammates, "Fellows, I'm just the backup goalie tonight but I want you all to know I'm very popular here in Philadelphia. I'll bet you I get a tremendous ovation when I skate out on the ice."

Sure enough, there was a big ovation when the teams took the ice . . . but of course it was for the Flyers, not for Smith.

Still, Smith skated around, saluting the crowd and waving at the fans, pretending *he* was the object of everybody's attention. It was pretty funny.

Later on in the game, Smith had to get serious. The Jets' starting goalie Pierre Hamel was injured and Smith took over in the Winnipeg goal. The crowd booed and jeered him, recalling his pre-game showboating. They jeered even louder when Smith gave up four goals and the Flyers rallied to win the game 5-4.

Days later, when the Flyer streak was fading into hockey history, coach Pat Quinn had a final comment on all the attention showered on the undefeated record.

"The streak was pure platinum," he said. "But the Stanley Cup . . . *that's* pure gold."

Rick MacLeish, one of hockey's finest skaters, played a big role in the streak.

Gordie was on four Stanley Cup teams and set dozens of records.

3 Gordie's Greatest Goals

My job as the world's most famous hockey puck is really quite simple. The referee drops me into the middle of a hockey game and players on two teams battle over me for the next sixty minutes. They pass me around and shoot me at the other team's goal and when I cross the red line painted on the ice between the two goal posts, it's a score. The team with the most scores, or goals, wins.

On every team, there are players who are more clever at scoring goals than others.

They control me with their sticks and pound my little rubber body with their heavy slap shots. Normally, I don't mind. It's all part of being a hockey puck. But some guys get carried away. They whack me around so hard, and zap me into the net so often, that I barely have time to catch my breath. It's a good thing I'm tough. Otherwise, I'm sure there'd be nights when I'd lose some of my bounce and they'd have to scrape me off the ice looking more like a rubbery meatball than a hockey puck.

One of the worst offenders is Gordie Howe. That old rascal has never been able to leave me alone. I think I've been patient. I've never complained before. But enough is enough. I look at it this way, kids. Gordie joined the NHL in 1946 and in the 1979-80 season he was still getting his kicks from knocking me past goalies. Thanks to my help, Gordie's scored over a thousand goals with three teams in two different leagues. I never dreamed he'd still be scoring big league goals well into his fifties. And as a two-time grandfather.

Another thing: he even plays hard with me in practice.

I know. Fans are going to say to me, "Pete, how can you put the rap on a great guy like Gordie Howe? He's been a marvel for over thirty years. And what a great sense of humor the man has."

Well, let me tell you about his sense of humor. Not long ago, Gordie took me out of the freezer one morning and threw me out on the practice rink. I'd had a tough game the night before and my eyes were barely open. But Gordie just laughed and said, "How about a little ride this morning, Pete?" With that, he slapped me high over the glass at the end of the rink and right out one of the exits. I landed in a snowbank outside the arena. Gordie had to fish me out with his stick. He was laughing so hard he could barely apologize. Now, is that any way for a puck to begin his working day?

There's never been another player quite like Gordie Howe. And when you've scored over a thousand goals in professional hockey it's almost impossible to single out one goal that's most memorable. But one day I read a list of ten of them on the sports page of *The Toronto Star*. Here's the list, just as it was printed. The ten are listed not in chronological order but in the order of their appeal to Number 9, the man who scored them.

1

Nov. 10, 1963, 15:06 of second period, at Detroit. Detroit 3, Montreal 0.

"The 545th to break Rocket Richard's record. I remember how the whole team was relieved. 'Now we can get back to playing hockey,' they said. It was against Canadiens and it was a short-handed goal. Bill Gadsby and Billy McNeill helped me set it up. Gadsby went down left wing and the defense had to play him. I beat Charlie Hodge from about the top of the circle."

At age 46, Gordie amazed the Soviets in 1974 when Team Canada (WHA players) met the Russian powerhouse in a turbulent eight-game series. With Team Canada trailing in game seven, and only two minutes to play, ageless Gordie drops his head to his chest. He knows his team has lost the series.

Gordie joined Detroit as a teenager in 1946.

2

Oct. 16, 1946, 13:39 of second period, at Detroit. Detroit 3, Toronto 3. Howe's first NHL game; he wore sweater No. 17, not his famous No. 9.

"My first one in the NHL, I remember it well. It was against Turk Broda. I was on a line with Sid Abel and Adam Brown. Brown's rebound hopped out and I popped it in. I remember another goal I got on the Turk. He came out to meet me and started backing up but he didn't realize he had lost his bearings. He backed up a couple of feet wide of the net. I swept around him and scored. The fans loved that one."

3

March 1, 1977, 1:31 of first period, at Houston. Houston 8, Phoenix 3.

"The 900th in Houston was one I got a lot of pleasure out of. Marty set it up so that balanced things out. Mark had assisted on my 800th. I cut between the defense and Marty hit me perfectly—right on my sore foot. I took my time shooting because I figured if I didn't score that Marty would kill me. I didn't get it where I wanted it either. I was trying to put it over the goal-keeper's bent elbow but he got a piece of it. It went in just the same."

4

March 14, 1962, 17:10 of second period, at New York. Rangers 3, Detroit 2.

"The 500th was against Gump Worsley and the Rangers, again while we were killing a penalty. It was a back-hander. I remember it was on a deke. I let it go as I cut around Doug Harvey."

5

Nov. 27, 1965, 16:10 of third period, at Montreal, Montreal 3, Detroit 2.

"The 600th was in Montreal. All I remember is standing to the right of Worsley. Gary Bergman gave the puck to Don McKenny and his shot came back out from behind the net. I shoved the puck in the net. Gump fished it out for me, handed it to me and said, 'Congratulations!'"

6

Dec. 13, 1958, 9:46 of third period, in Montreal. Montreal 2, Detroit 2.

"I got my 400th in Montreal also. I was battling Maurice Richard in the corner and the puck was knocked back to the point. Pete Goegan fired a shot at Jacques Plante. It would have missed the net but Richard, who had stuck with me out of the corner, lifted my stick. The puck hit it and deflected into the net."

7

Oct. 27, 1963, 11:04 of third period, at Detroit. Montreal 6, Detroit 4.

"The 544th, which tied Richard's record, was in Detroit against the Canadiens. The Canadiens got caught on a line change. I can still see Henri Richard standing in the gate as I steered Bruce MacGregor's pass behind Worsley."

8

Jan. 17, 1974, 5:46 of first period, at Houston. Houston 7, Vancouver 4.

"The 800th was in Houston. It was against a kid I used to tutor in hockey school, Peter Donnelly. It was a rebound of Mark's and I jammed it past Donnelly."

9

Sept. 25, 1973. Four WHA teams participated, in New York, in a round-robin game during which each team played a period against each of the others. Houston got in the game in the third period and twenty-one seconds later Howe scored, against New England.

"The first goal I scored for Houston was mighty pleasing. Remember, I had been out of the game for two years. We were playing this round-robin in Madison Square Garden and I was on a line with Mark and Jimmy Sherritt. Thirteen seconds after the game started I scored a goal against New England. It was a doubt remover." (Howe's memory was eight seconds out.)

Gordie scored over a thousand big league goals. Brother Vic scored just three in a brief career with the Rangers in the fifties. What a brother combination!

10

Sept. 23, 1974, at 4:20 of first period, at Vancouver. Canada 5, Soviet Union 5.

"One I got against the Soviets in Vancouver was satisfying. I got a goal and two assists on Tretiak in that game. They picked me as the star of the game and gave me a TV set even though Bobby Hull got three goals. It was Mark, I think, who gave me a pass. The Soviet defense tried to pinch me—they're quick and good staggerers—but before they closed I wristed it in."

One goal Gordie didn't have on his list was his 700th. He may not recall the goal but his former teammate, Alex Delvecchio, remembers it vividly.

Gordie finished his 32-year career with the
Hartford Whalers.

18

"Gordie scored his 700th in Pittsburgh," recalls Delvecchio. "I remember giving the puck to Frank Mahovlich. Frank passed it to Gordie and he blasted it past Les Binkley, the Penguins' netminder. The thing is, he wasn't supposed to score it in Pittsburgh. He was supposed to score it in Detroit. They had 700 balloons ready to float down when he scored. So, before the next Red Wing game, they asked us to re-enact the goal with Gordie putting the puck into the empty net. Would you believe it took us three tries before we clicked on the play? I think Gordie goofed it up deliberately, just to have a little fun."

Have a little fun? That was always Gordie's approach to hockey. And when I think about it, I never really minded when he had a little fun at my expense.

Some fans get very confused when it comes to Gordie's goal scoring records. And no wonder. Gordie talks about scoring his 800th career goal in Houston and the NHL says he scored his 800th in Hartford.

Let's try to set the record straight. The NHL makes a clear distinction between NHL records and WHA records. So while Gordie did score his 800th *career* goal for Houston in 1974, he was only credited with

Sons Marty (left) and Mark (right) helped make Gordie's dream come true. More than anything, he wanted to play with them.

his 800th *NHL* goal in March 1980 for Hartford. That goal came during a game against the St. Louis Blues on a five-foot shot that eluded goaltender Mike Liut.

After the 1979-80 season, Gordie announced his retirement from professional hockey after thirty-two years in the game.

He played twenty-five years with the Detroit Red Wings, retired for two years, then joined the Houston Aeros of the WHA to play with his two sons, Mark and Marty. Howe's career spanned five decades in which he scored over two thousand points in more than two thousand games.

On December 7, 1977, he zapped me past Birmingham goalie John Garrett to become the first player to score a thousand career goals in pro hockey (regular season and playoff goals).

Most players have to wait four or five years after retiring to become a candidate for the Hockey Hall of Fame. Old Gordie was still playing pro hockey eight years after he was elected to the Hockey Hall.

Gordie (wearing helmet) led the NHL in scoring six times.

Gordie's Complete Record

HOWE, GORDON
Born, Floral, Saskatchewan, March 31, 1928.
Right wing. Shoots right. 6', 205 lbs.
Last amateur club: Saskatoon Lions Club Juveniles.

Season	Club	League	Regular Schedule					Playoffs				
			GP	G	A	TP	PIM*	GP	G	A	TP	PIM
1945-46	Omaha	USHL	51	22	26	48	53	6	2	1	3	15
1946-47	Detroit	NHL	58	7	15	22	52	5	0	0	0	18
1947-48	Detroit	NHL	60	16	28	44	63	10	1	1	2	11
1948-49a	Detroit	NHL	40	12	25	37	57	11	*8	3	*11	19
1949-50a	Detroit	NHL	70	35	33	68	69	1	0	0	0	7
1950-51bc	Detroit	NHL	70	*43	*43	*86	74	6	4	3	7	4
1951-52bcd	Detroit	NHL	70	*47	39	*86	78	8	2	*5	*7	2
1952-53bcd	Detroit	NHL	70	*49	*46	*95	57	6	2	5	7	2
1953-54bc	Detroit	NHL	70	33	*48	*81	109	12	4	5	9	*31
1954-55	Detroit	NHL	64	29	33	62	68	11	*9	11	*20	24
1955-56a	Detroit	NHL	70	38	41	79	100	10	3	9	12	8
1956-57bcd	Detroit	NHL	70	*44	45	*89	72	5	2	5	7	6
1957-58bd	Detroit	NHL	64	33	44	77	40	4	1	1	2	0
1958-59a	Detroit	NHL	70	32	46	78	57	....	....	....	....	....
1959-60bd	Detroit	NHL	70	28	45	73	46	6	1	5	6	4
1960-61a	Detroit	NHL	64	23	49	72	30	11	4	11	*15	10
1961-62a	Detroit	NHL	70	33	44	77	54	....	....	....	....	....
1962-63bcd	Detroit	NHL	70	*38	48	*86	100	11	7	9	*16	22
1963-64a	Detroit	NHL	69	26	47	73	70	14	*9	10	*19	16
1964-65a	Detroit	NHL	70	29	47	76	104	7	4	2	6	20
1965-66b	Detroit	NHL	70	29	46	75	83	12	4	6	10	12
1966-67ae	Detroit	NHL	69	25	40	65	53	....	....	....	....	....
1967-68b	Detroit	NHL	74	39	43	82	53	....	....	....	....	....
1968-69b	Detroit	NHL	76	44	59	103	58	....	....	....	....	....
1969-70b	Detroit	NHL	76	31	40	71	58	4	2	0	2	2
1970-71	Detroit	NHL	63	23	29	52	38	....	....	....	....	....
1971-72	Did Not Play.											
1972-73	Did Not Play.											
1973-74	Houston	WHA	70	31	69	100	46	13	3	*14	17	34
1974-75	Houston	WHA	75	34	65	99	84	13	8	12	20	20
1975-76	Houston	WHA	78	32	70	102	76	17	4	8	12	31
1976-77	Houston	WHA	62	24	44	68	57	11	5	3	8	11
1977-78	New England	WHA	76	34	62	96	85	14	5	5	10	15
1978-79	New England	WHA	58	19	24	43	51	10	3	1	4	4
1979-80	Hartford	NHL	80	15	26	41	42	3	1	1	2	2
	NHL Totals		1,767	801	1,049	1,850	1,685	157	68	92	160	220
	WHA Totals		419	174	334	508	399	78	28	43	71	115

a Second All-Star Team (right wing).
b First All-Star Team (right wing).
c Won Art Ross Trophy.
d Won Hart Memorial Trophy.
e Won Lester Patrick Trophy.

*GP = Games played.
G = Goals.
A = Assists.
TP = Total points.
PIM = Penalties in minutes.

On Darryl's big night, some people thought I was glued to his stick . . . until he shot, that is.

4 Sittler's Scoring Spree

Because a hockey puck takes funny bounces and the game is played on ice, any single game can produce a number of surprises.

Take the night of February 7, 1976, at Maple Leaf Gardens in Toronto, for example.

The Boston Bruins met the Toronto Maple Leafs and I was paying particular attention to several of the Bruins. At least three of them were capable of giving that game special meaning. Gerry Cheevers, the Boston goalie, had just returned from playing in the WHA, and I figured him for a big performance. But Cheevers was not in top shape so Boston coach Don Cherry started rookie Dave Reece in goal against the Leafs.

Darryl said, "There's no way I can ever explain why things happened the way they did that night."

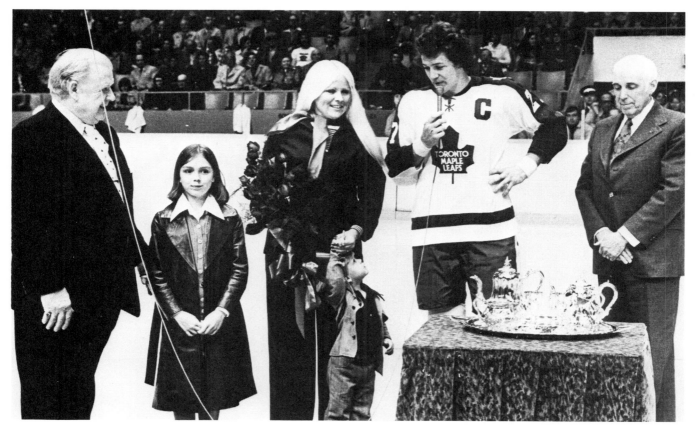

After his record performance, Leaf owner Harold Ballard presented Darryl with a $7,500 antique silver tea service. That's Darryl's wife Wendy next to him and son Ryan in front.

The Bruins' veteran winger, Johnny Bucyk, had a chance to move into second place among the all-time NHL scorers that night. I was rooting for Johnny. He always played hard but clean and he always treated me with respect.

Then there was Jean Ratelle, another Bruin veteran. Jean was gunning for his 350th NHL goal. If he got it, he would become the eighteenth player in NHL history to reach that plateau.

To add to the interest, the Bruins were on a seven-game winning streak. So all eyes were on the Boston players when they took the ice that night.

But the fellow we should have been watching was Leaf captain Darryl Sittler. All the other players that night were completely overshadowed by the Leafs' number 27.

In all of the other games that had been played up until that night, 13,528 of them, no player had ever collected more than eight points in a single game. But that night a lot of records went POOF!

Sittler, the leader of the Leafs, collected an eye-popping ten points in Toronto's 11-4 rout of the Bruins. I'm sure some fans thought I must have been taped to Darryl's stick the way I went around with him that night. He knocked me into the Boston net six times and assisted his teammates on four other goals. It was a game Darryl will always remember and Dave Reece would like to forget.

Sittler started his scoring spree against Reece when he assisted on two Toronto goals in the first period. He really got rolling in the second period with three goals plus two assists. In the third, he

Darryl's first NHL goal was one for the book. It was not only his first big league score but it was the first NHL goal allowed by rookie Red Wing goalie Smokey McLeod.

banged in three more goals to complete the greatest individual performance in NHL history.

Now, Maple Leaf Gardens is not the noisiest arena in the league. Fans there seldom whoop it up the way they do in many other NHL rinks. But that night! After Darryl scored his ninth point he received a tremendous ovation. And when he scored his sixth goal and tenth point I was sure the roof was going to fly off.

Later he told me, "Pete, the thing I'll always remember about that night is the applause they gave me. It's something no player would ever forget."

Darryl was quick to praise his teammates for their role in the point spree.

"It was a night when every time I had

the puck something seemed to happen," he said. "But it couldn't have happened without some of my teammates playing at the top of their game. Borje Salming made a couple of super rushes that night to set up two of my goals. My wingers, Lanny McDonald and Errol Thompson, were flying. They both handled the puck extremely well and created plenty of holes for me. It's funny, I've worked just as hard in other games without scoring a single point. There is no way I can ever explain why things happened the way they did that night.

"Some of my goals were good goals but a couple of them were soft. One or two bounced in off the goalie's pad or trickled through his skates. They weren't classic goals. The sixth goal, and the tenth point,

Later that same year, Darryl scored the winning goal in overtime to win the Canada Cup. Team Canada defeated Czechoslovakia in a thriller at the Montreal Forum.

bounced off the leg of defenseman Brad Park and then skidded through the legs of Reece. I really felt sorry for Reece. I hate to think I was instrumental in finishing a player's career but I don't think he was ever the same after that night at the Gardens. He slipped into obscurity after that."

Sittler's performance saw him smash two league records and tie a third. He also set four team marks.

Darryl's dash into the record book produced the following: (1) most points in one game, ten. The previous record, eight, was held by two Montreal Canadiens, Maurice Richard (in 1944) and Bert Olmstead (in 1954). (2) Three goals in each of two successive periods. No NHL player ever had accomplished this. (3) Most points in one period, five. Sittler's three goals and two assists in the second period tied an NHL record shared by Chicago's Les Cunningham and Max Bentley and Leo Labine of Boston.

Sittler became only the eighth player to score six goals in a game and only one, Joe Malone of Quebec Bulldogs, scored seven, the all-time NHL record. But Malone scored his away back in 1920, long before the so-called "modern era" of hockey.

Sittler had another big night that season in the playoffs. Playing against Philadelphia and goalie Bernie Parent, Sittler scored five goals to tie a playoff record for most goals in a game.

"Bernie seldom gives up five goals in a game," Sittler told reporters, "and never five to any one player. But it happened. Don't ask me how. I took eight shots and five of them went in. What more can I say? Better ask Peter Puck if you want to know how."

Gee, I didn't know how either. The hockey world is just a blur to me when I'm en route to the net. Especially when Sittler shoots me.

But I can't end this story yet. I began by telling you about Johnny Bucyk and Jean Ratelle of the Bruins and how they were aiming at some milestones during that memorable night at Maple Leaf Gardens.

Bucyk played well and collected the points he needed to move into second place (behind Gordie Howe) among all-time scorers. And Ratelle scored one goal and became the eighteenth player to reach the 350 goal plateau during regular season play.

Darryl and his son Ryan. Darryl believes it's a good idea to start training at an early age.

After playing half the night, I was an imp on the limp. I was a puck looking for a pillow.

5 These Fellows Played Hockey All Night

I'll bet you don't know anyone who would play hockey all night. Or even half the night. Hockey's fun, but how many players would play the game hour after hour, stubbornly refusing to go home and get a good night's sleep until a winning goal was scored and a championship decided?

Come to think of it, I know a lot of fellows who would do that—and did. More than once. What's more, a few thousand fans stayed up until the wee small hours *watching* them do it.

Let me tell you about two of the longest games ever played in hockey. Naturally, I played a pretty big role in both of them.

On April 3, 1933, referee Odie Cleghorn carried me to center ice at Maple Leaf Gardens to face me off in a big game between the Maple Leafs and the Boston Bruins.

"I hope it's a good, fast game, Pete," said Odie. "The winning team has to catch a train for New York where they'll meet the Rangers in the Stanley Cup finals beginning tomorrow night. If the game goes late, they won't get much sleep."

Much sleep! It turned out they hardly slept at all. And here's why.

The game, which began promptly at 8:30, was a tight checking, defensive struggle with both clubs cautiously waiting for the break that would give them the first goal.

There was no score in the first period and no score in the second. Then, with fourteen minutes gone in the third period, Boston's Alex Smith raced in and slammed me into the Toronto net. But referee Cleghorn blew his whistle and disallowed the goal. Offside, he ruled.

The Boston players grumbled while the Leafs breathed a sigh of relief. The game continued and the teams finished the sixty minutes of regulation time without a goal being scored.

Neither goalie would let me cross the goal line. "Watch it, fella! I'll report you to the S.P.C.H.P. — the Society for Prevention of Cruelty to Hockey Pucks."

Bruneteau's winning shot stopped the clock after 176 minutes and 30 seconds — the longest game ever.

That really didn't surprise anyone. The teams were so evenly matched that this was the fourth time in the five-game series that overtime was required to settle matters.

The first twenty minutes of overtime were played and there was still no score. Neither goalie, Lorne Chabot for the Leafs and Tiny Thompson for the Bruins, would let me cross the goal line. There was another overtime period. And another.

Midnight came and went and the players struggled on. The early edition of the morning paper appeared in the arena and fans chuckled over references to the "big playoff game played *last* night."

In the fourth overtime period, the Leafs thought they'd won it. King Clancy broke away with Joe Primeau. Clancy took Primeau's pass and scored. But again, referee Cleghorn waved his arms and disallowed the goal.

"Mr. Clancy, you were offside on the play," he ruled.

The cheers of the Leaf fans turned to groans and referee Cleghorn instantly became the most unpopular man in Toronto. But he stuck out his chin and said, "Let's play hockey."

By the end of the fourth overtime period, league officials were in a quandary. NHL president Frank Calder called the teams aside and said, "Listen, men, we've got to figure out a way to end this game."

Someone suggested the game be stopped and resumed the next night. "We can't do that," ruled the president. "One of these clubs has got to be in New York for the game there. And that game is just a few hours away now."

"Why don't we take both goalies out and play without them," someone else suggested. "That should soon settle things. After all, they've stopped about two hundred shots between them."

But that idea was quickly rejected.

Manager Conn Smythe of the Leafs talked with manager Art Ross of the Bruins. They decided to flip a coin to decide a winner. But their players protested.

"We don't want this game settled by a coin toss," said the players. Let's play on and settle it on the ice."

And that's what they did.

Milkmen were getting up to make their morning deliveries when the sixth overtime period got underway. Some fans went home but most stayed, excited to be in the stands when hockey history was being made.

Four minutes into the sixth overtime, the Bruins' great star Eddie Shore passed the puck to his teammate Joe Lamb. But the Leafs' Andy Blair anticipated Shore's move and quickly intercepted. Blair didn't hold on to me. He sent me skimming onto the stick of little Ken Doraty, a right winger. Doraty streaked in on goal and fired me past Thompson, just inside the goal post.

What an explosion of sound! The Leafs had won and tiny Doraty, at 5' 6" and 150 lbs, was the hero of the game.

His mates tried to lift him on their shoulders but he would have no part of that. Perhaps he figured they would throw him in the air in their excitement and forget to catch him on the way down.

So the game ended after 164 minutes and 46 seconds, at 4:46 of the sixth overtime period. During the contest, Toronto outshot Boston 119 to 93.

Some of the fans didn't get home until dawn and most were convinced there'd never be another game like it.

You are probably wondering how the Leafs made out in their game with the New York Rangers that followed the longest game in league history. The Leafs left by train right after the game and arrived in New York just in time for the playoff clash with the Rangers.

Little Ken Doraty was a big man for the Leafs in the sixth overtime period.

As you can imagine, they were dead-tired and no match for the well-rested New York team who won the game and eventually the series and the Stanley Cup.

I must say I agreed with the Toronto fans who witnessed the longest game played to that time, the ones who said there'd never be another one like it.

But we were all wrong.

Just three seasons later, there was another playoff game played in Montreal between the Montreal Maroons and the Detroit Red Wings. It was the first game of a semi-final series. The goalies were Norm Smith of Detroit and my old friend Lorne Chabot, who had left Toronto to join the Maroons. If Chabot had known what he was in for—another night of hockey like the one he'd survived, and won, in Toronto—he might have packed a few sandwiches and a thermos of coffee and stashed them in his goal net.

Chabot and Smith stopped dozens of shots and their stingy behavior kept all the other players off the scoresheet through sixty minutes of regulation play.

Then the clubs struggled through one, two, three, four, five periods of overtime.

Finally, after 176 minutes and 30 seconds of playoff hockey, in the sixth overtime period, an energetic player for Detroit named Modère (Mud) Bruneteau trapped me on his stick about twenty-five feet out from the Montreal net. He zapped me past Chabot and the game was over. Strangely enough, it was Bruneteau's very first play-off game. He had played a few games with Detroit during the regular season but spent most of the year in the minors. It was his biggest hockey thrill. Bruneteau's name is still in the record books as the man who scored the winning goal in the longest hockey game ever played.

Poor Chabot. After being the winning goalie in the marathon game in Toronto, he now suffered the agony of losing in an even longer game in Montreal.

But then, look at it this way. It could have been worse. He could have lost both games.

"You can be the hero of the playoffs, Bill . . . so take your best shot."

6 Bill Barilko's Final Goal

I love the playoffs, when Stanley Cup fever grabs every hockey fan and won't let go.

One playoff goal I'll never forget was scored by Bill Barilko of the Toronto Maple Leafs back in the spring of 1951.

It was the final goal scored in one of hockey's most incredible playoff series—a series in which every game required overtime—and it was the final goal in Bill Barilko's promising career.

That season of 1950-51 rightfully belonged to Detroit. The Red Wings soared to the top of the NHL and finished the regular season with a record 101 points. The Leafs finished the seventy-game schedule with ninety-five points, an all time record for a Toronto team.

In the semi-finals, the Leafs met Boston and knocked them out of the Stanley Cup hunt without too much trouble.

Meanwhile, a stunning upset took place in the battle between Detroit and Montreal for a berth into the finals. Montreal had finished thirty-six points back of Detroit in the final standings and everybody figured the Habs would be pushovers for the powerful Red Wings. After all, the Wings had twenty-three-year-old Gordie Howe playing on a line with Ted Lindsay and Sid Abel, a trio so skillful at scoring they were named the "Production Line."

But Montreal had Rocket Richard and when the playoff pressure was on, nobody performed like the Rocket.

In game one, he slammed me into the Red Wing net after more than an hour of overtime play to give Montreal a 3-2 victory. And just to prove it was no fluke, he did the same thing in game two, sinking the Wings with another overtime goal. Both these games were played in Detroit, where the Wings had lost only three games all season.

Gordie Howe rallied the Wings in games three and four in Montreal and the series was tied when the clubs returned to Detroit. But Montreal made it three in a row at the Olympia when Boom Boom Geoffrion, a young player who has been credited with introducing the slapshot, scored the winner with a sizzler from fifty-five feet out.

Back on home ice in Montreal, the Canadiens eliminated the shocked Red Wings by winning the sixth game 3-2.

That set the stage for a final showdown between two old rivals, Montreal and Toronto, with the Stanley Cup waiting for the winners.

It has to rank as one of the most memorable Stanley Cup finals in hockey history. It lasted five games and every one of those games went into sudden death overtime.

The Leafs were heavy favorites because they had handled Montreal easily during the regular season, losing only two of the fourteen games played between the two clubs.

The first game was played in Toronto, and with the score tied 2-2 near the end of the game, I was sure Rocket Richard was going to score the winner. He zoomed in from right wing on an unprotected Leaf net. But when he shot, Bill Barilko, a husky young Toronto defenseman, dove frantically in front of me and blocked the shot. It was a courageous move by Barilko and I saw Richard glare at him as if to say, "My friend, I don't know how you stopped that shot but it saved the Leaf bacon. I hope you don't have any more moves like that up your sleeve."

As it turned out, Barilko's move was a game-saving play, because Toronto's Sid Smith rapped me into the Montreal goal six minutes into the overtime to give the Leafs a 3-2 victory.

The second game was also tied 2-2 at the end of regulation play. In the overtime, Richard sank the Leafs 3-2 with a goal and this time he didn't have to worry about a kid named Barilko diving in front of his shot.

In game three, it was Toronto captain Ted Kennedy's turn. He came through with an overtime goal to beat Montreal 2-1. It took another overtime score to decide a winner in game four. It was Harry Watson of the Leafs who came through in this game, clinching another Toronto win with a score after 5:15 of extra play.

Talk about tension! Never before in Stanley Cup play had four straight games been decided by overtime goals. And it wasn't over yet.

The series also set a record for abrupt endings. None of the overtime periods had gone beyond six minutes of play.

Game five was the most dramatic of them all. For the first time in the series, it appeared certain that Montreal would win in regulation time. The Canadiens were leading 2-1 in the final minute of play. That's when Toronto coach Joe Primeau waved his goalie to the bench and sent out an extra attacker. The Leaf net was empty.

Barilko, racing in from the blueline, took Meeker's pass and slapped the puck past McNeil.

The Leafs moved the puck into the Montreal zone. They worked it around until Tod Sloan was in the clear. A good pass put it right on Sloan's stick and with just thirty-two seconds to play he zapped me into the Montreal net, tying the game 2-2.

Bedlam broke loose in Maple Leaf Gardens as 14,577 screaming fans went delirious. Papers and programs thudded onto the ice. The band played as loudly as it could, and it was several minutes before the referee could face off the puck for the final few seconds of regulation play.

Play resumed and the teams finished regulation time with no further score. They went to their dressing rooms to rest and prepare for an unprecedented fifth consecutive overtime. None of them had ever been through a tension-packed series quite like this one.

That night of April 21, 1951, and the few thrilling minutes of overtime play that decided the series, will live forever in the memories of Leaf fans. Like the first four games, it didn't take much extra time to decide a winner.

The Leafs pressed right from the faceoff. Howie Meeker and Harry Watson hounded the Montreal defenders and kept the puck in the Canadiens' zone. They fired me at

Montreal goalie Gerry McNeil a couple of times but he blocked their efforts to score.

Then Meeker's persistent checking paid off. When I rolled off the boards behind the Montreal goal Howie trapped me with his stick. Then he slipped me out into the slot area because he spotted Bill Barilko racing in from the blue line. It was a perfect pass and a perfect play. Barilko, under a full head of steam, took Meeker's relay and whacked me at McNeil. McNeil leaped at the rising shot but it was just out of reach. I landed high in the net and the game was over.

Fans and players leaped over the boards. The Leaf players hugged and slapped each other and danced around in the kind of ritual that is a familiar part of every victory celebration. Two Leafs, Cal Gardner and Bill Juzda, hoisted Barilko onto

"Look, Pete, we've won the cup. Thanks for heading straight for the net."

Mr. Conn Smythe, the Leaf owner, congratulates Bill as Joe Klukay and Harry Watson grin their endorsement.

their shoulders. The curly-haired hero laughed and waved at the crowd.

Suddenly, someone spotted coach Joe Primeau in the crowd. The players grabbed Primeau and hoisted him up to shoulder height. Again, there was a standing ovation. Primeau had a special reason for celebrating. He became the first coach in history to complete hockey's coaching grand slam—winning the Memorial, Allan and Stanley Cups.

But there's a sad footnote to this story about Bill Barilko's famous goal. It turned out to be the final goal of his NHL career.

A few weeks later, he and a friend, Dr. Henry Hudson, went on a fishing trip to Northern Ontario. They flew to a remote spot in Dr. Hudson's private plane. The plane disappeared and a massive search party was organized to comb the northland.

Conn Smythe, manager of the Leafs, offered a $10,000 reward when the mystery of Barilko's disappearance began to deepen.

Searchers spent thousands of hours combing the rugged terrain near Cochrane, but not a trace of the plane was found. The reward offer expired on January 1, 1952.

The mystery produced some disturbing rumors. Some folks in Kirkland Lake thought the disappearance might have been tied in to some gold smuggling hanky panky. But the dense forest knew better.

On June 6, 1962—eleven years after the plane disappeared—the forest gave up the remains of a twisted, rotting Fairchild. Inside were the skeletons of two men.

Bill Barilko and Dr. Hudson had been killed instantly in the crash. Some say engine failure caused the accident, others figure the plane was overloaded with fish.

Bill Barilko is gone, but not forgotten.

The Flyers played bump and thump hockey. And it paid off in a Stanley Cup parade watched by millions.

7 Flyers Win in '74

I was leafing through my hockey scrapbook recently when I came across a clipping of a game played in Philadelphia in the spring of 1974.

There's no reason why you should remember the date, May 19, 1974. But I do. It was the day the Philadelphia Flyers became the first expansion team to win the Stanley Cup. The Flyers' unexpected triumph touched off the wildest celebration I'd ever seen. The U.S. Olympic hockey team's victory at Lake Placid in 1980 may have been toasted by more millions of Americans from coast-to-coast, but for concentrated cheering, backslapping and good old hero worship, there was nothing like Philadelphia in '74.

As you might expect, I was right in the middle of that frantic final game that decided the Stanley Cup.

Clarke, a diabetic from Flin Flon, Manitoba, came to Philadelphia to win fame and fortune with the Flyers.

The Flyers, thanks to Bobby Clarke's leadership, Bernie Parent's brilliant goaltending and Fred Shero's coaching, turned a city renowned for its losers into a city of ecstatic winners on that warm May afternoon at the Spectrum.

I'd even credit Kate Smith with an assist. When she made a personal appearance to sing "God Bless America" before the game, the Flyers were ready to battle the Boston Bruins into submission.

Philadelphia sports fans touched off an incredible celebration right after the Flyers blanked the Bruins 1-0 in the sixth and final game of the Stanley Cup playoffs.

It was a long time between championships. The last Philadelphia winners were the basketball Warriors, winners of the NBA title in 1967. But the spontaneous, madcap victory party to salute the Flyers made any dimly-remembered celebration for the Warriors seem like a child's birthday party by comparison.

Bobby Clarke was kind enough to invite me along for the Flyers' victory parade the following day. I must say I was astounded at the size of the crowd.

We all got into open convertibles for the long drive down Broad and Chestnut Streets while some two million fans screamed their delight. They tossed confetti and kisses and swarmed around our slow-moving vehicles. And when the Stanley Cup was held aloft, the crowd roared its approval.

Later, the cup was put on display in the main branch of a large city bank where it attracted 15,000 viewers on the very first day it was unveiled. A steady stream of Flyer hockey fans, many of them showing the after-effects of their partying, filed past the showcase housing hockey's most famous trophy. They came to admire and photograph the reward that goes annually to the world's top professional hockey team.

Let me try to explain how the Flyers rose to the top of the pack. More than anything,

Bernie Parent was magnificent in goal and won the Conn Smythe Trophy as Most Valuable Player of the playoffs.

it was teamwork, desire and dedication that brought the cup to Philadelphia. The hard work started in training camp months earlier and it continued on throughout the regular season of 1973-74. The Flyers finished the schedule with 112 points, and captured their division championship.

When the Flyers whipped the Bruins in Philadelphia to clinch the title late in the season, it marked their first win over Boston in five years. Thousands of orange and black balloons, stashed high in the rafters above the Spectrum, floated down over the jubilant crowd, who stamped their feet and shouted "We're Number One. We're Number One."

Dave Schultz was the biggest of the "Bullies" and spent more time in the "cooler" than Peter Puck.

Then came the playoffs. The Atlanta Flames, winners of a playoff berth in only their second season in the league, lost the first two games to the Flyers in the quarter-finals at the Spectrum. The two teams journeyed back to Atlanta where excitement of a different kind awaited them.

Game three at the Omni was interrupted by a bench-clearing brawl plus a disputed Philadelphia goal. The puck obviously hit the crossbar but was ruled a goal. Dan Bouchard, the Atlanta goalie, was irate. He shoved referee Dave Newell and swung his big goal stick at linesman Neil Armstrong. The Flyers won again.

It was after this affair that Fred Shero, Philadelphia's coach, went for a walk in a tough section of Atlanta. Reports are vague but Shero apparently met up with some unsavory characters. The only thing he remembered was waking up in his hotel room feeling sore and bruised all over. With Shero recuperating from what was called a "vicious mugging," assistant coach Mike Nykoluk handled the team in game four which the Flyers won to sweep the series.

While Boston was busy eliminating first Toronto and then Chicago, the Flyers moved on to meet the New York Rangers, winners over Montreal in a quarter final matchup.

The semi-final thriller between the Flyers and the Rangers was a home-ice series all the way. Both clubs were invincible in front of their home-town fans. As a result, the Flyers had the extra home game. They won the deciding game and advanced to the finals.

After disposing of New York, the Flyers found themselves right where everybody predicted they would be—facing the powerful Boston Bruins in the Stanley Cup finals.

The series opened in Boston and it was superstar Bobby Orr who scored a dramatic third period goal with only twenty-two seconds left to play. That score carried the Bruins to a 3-2 victory.

Then Bobby Clarke played the hero's role in game two. He took an overtime pass from bearded Bill Flett and fired me right at Boston goalie Gilles Gilbert, who went down. Clarke saw me spin away from Gilbert. He snared me on his stick, spun around and drove me into the net. Flyers 3, Boston 2.

The Flyers were even stronger back on home ice. They took two games in a row by scores of 4-1 and 4-2 to grab a commanding lead in the series. But the Bruins weren't through yet. Back in Boston, Bobby Orr took personal command in game five. He scored two goals and set up a third. The Flyers couldn't touch him.

The Flyers were involved in many brawls during the 1973-74 season.

So the series moved back to Philadelphia. Kate Smith was there in person. Kate is a lovely lady who's been singing songs on radio and television for many years. She was the Flyers' good luck charm all season long. Almost invariably, when Kate sang "God Bless America" before a Flyers' home game, Philadelphia would win. Her record up to this big game with Boston was 36-3-1.

The Governor of the State of Pennsylvania was there . . . the mayor of Philadelphia . . . everybody.

When Kate strolled out to center ice and sang her song under a spotlight she received a standing ovation that lasted for several minutes. Nobody knew it at the time but that ovation would be topped by an even bigger one for the Flyers before the afternoon was over.

The first goal of the game came at 14:47 of the first period. Philadelphia's Rick MacLeish scored it, his thirteenth of the playoffs. Little did I know, or anyone else at the time, that it would be the only goal scored in the game—in fact, the final goal of the series and the season.

The Philadelphia goalie, Bernie Parent, was magnificent. He stopped me every time the Bruins drove me in his direction. And late in the game, I'm sure he winked at me as if to say, "If you've got any notion of getting past me today Pete, forget it."

Then, with only a couple of minutes to play, when the fans in the steaming Spec-

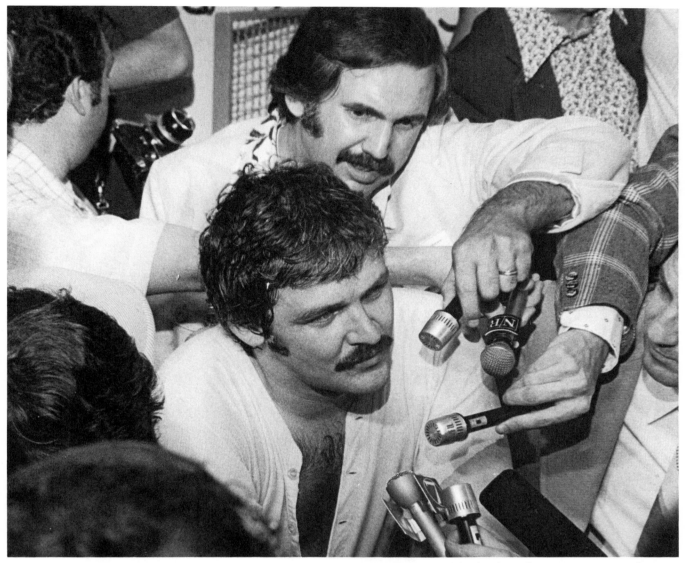
Parent said winning the cup was more important than being named MVP.

trum and millions more watching on television across North America were bracing themselves for what looked like a smashing conclusion, the referee blew his whistle and signaled a penalty for holding to Boston's Bobby Orr. Orr was caught wrestling Clarke to the ice when it appeared as if Clarke might break away alone. It was a crushing call against the Bruins.

The penalty to Orr dashed all Boston hopes. Without Orr, their chances for a tie evaporated.

Moments later, the final buzzer sounded. The Spectrum erupted. The Flyers were champions at last, a hard working gang of muscular, dedicated skaters who had achieved a hockey "first."

Not only were they the first team in Philadelphia history to reign as hockey's champions, they were the first of all the expansion teams to win the Stanley Cup.

"You're not going to throw me in with the Canadiens, are you, ref? Those guys grab me and never let me go."

8 Five in a Row in the Fifties

From 1955 through 1960, the Montreal Canadiens were the greatest team in hockey. They won one Stanley Cup after another, and with players like Plante, Harvey, the two Richards, Beliveau, Moore and Geoffrion in the lineup, they were often described as "the perfect hockey team."

In the spring of 1959, after the Canadiens had won their fourth straight Stanley Cup to set a record for consecutive cup wins, I

congratulated their coach, Toe Blake.

"Thanks a lot, Pete," he said. "To me, this was our club's finest hour. We were out to break the three straight Cup record we shared with Toronto."

When I reminded Blake that Boston's Lynn Patrick had recently declared, "Time is catching up with Montreal. Their reign is nearly over," and that Toronto's Stafford Smythe had told the Habs, "Take a good look at the Cup, fellows. It'll be the last time you'll see it for awhile", the Montreal coach just chuckled.

"That's just envy, Pete. I hear a lot of guff about how we're getting older. But don't worry about the Canadiens. We'll be back next year and I don't see why we can't make it five in a row."

During the 1959-60 season Blake's team was just as powerful as he said it would be. At the end of the regular season the Canadiens finished on top with 92 points compared with second place Toronto's 79.

With the playoffs about to get underway, everybody was asking the same question, "Was there any team in hockey strong enough to stop Montreal?"

The Canadiens' first playoff opponents were the Chicago Black Hawks. With scoring champion Bobby Hull sidelined with an abscessed tonsil and Stan Mikita out with a badly swollen eye, the Hawks were at a disadvantage in game one. They lost 4-3. The second game went to Montreal by the same score but it was accomplished the hard way, in overtime. Veteran Doug Harvey, the great defenseman, scored at 8:38 of the first overtime period to put Montreal two games ahead in the series. Earlier, Chicago's Bill Hay had forced the overtime with a goal sixty-two seconds from the end of regulation time.

A one-sided 4-0 victory clinched game three for Montreal with a makeshift line of Ralph Backstrom, Donnie Marshall and Bill Hicke leading the attack. Infuriated Black Hawk fans bombarded the ice with debris, including sandbags and paper, as the disorganized home club failed to get a shot on Jacques Plante in the final ten minutes of play. A 2-0 win on March 31 swept Chicago aside and thrust Montreal into the finals. Toe Blake picked his Vezina trophy-winning goalie Jacques Plante as the big man in the Montreal victory. Earlier in the season, Plante had provided many columns of sports page copy when he donned a face mask for the first time.

Jean Beliveau, one of the most popular players of all time, was the inspirational leader of the Habs.

Meanwhile, Toronto met Detroit in the other semi-final series. Goals by Gordie Howe and Len Haley provided the Red Wings with a 2-1 opening game triumph.

With big league hockey players, money speaks louder than words. That's what Toronto coach Punch Imlach had in mind before the second game of the series. Imlach carefully stacked up $1,250 in the middle of the Leafs' dressing room floor during the pre-game warmup. When the Leafs tramped into the room, they read a message on the blackboard: "Take a good look at the money on the floor. That represents the difference between winning and losing." With Larry Regan providing the spark, the Leafs skated to a 4-2 victory over the Wings.

The Leafs may have had big money in mind—let's call it a playoff payoff—when they skated out for the next game in Detroit. The game went into three overtime periods before Frank Mahovlich scored his second goal in a 5-4 Leaf victory. After Johnny Bower robbed Gordie Howe on what appeared to be a sure goal in the overtime, Howe skated over to his off-season fishing companion and said: "When we get out in the boat next summer, you're going in the lake."

The Wings were sharper than the Leafs at every position but goal in game four. Detroit got the winning goal from Jerry Melnyk after 1:54 of overtime on a power play. Toronto's Ron Stewart was in the penalty box.

When asked for a comment prior to the fifth game, veteran Leaf Allan Stanley said: "Every year the story crops up that my legs are gone, that I'm too tired to be effective. Heck, I might just beat those Wings myself." The next night Stanley cut

The Rocket's eyes blazed when he neared the goal. In the fifties, he was hockey's greatest scorer.

loose with two goals and assisted on two others in a 5-4 Leaf victory. Stanley had scored only three goals in forty previous Stanley Cup games.

In game six the Leafs trailed Detroit 2-1 going into the third period. Imlach tossed a challenge at them: "You say you can handle any line Sid Abel tosses at you. Well, let's see you do it." The Leafs did, scoring three times for a 4-2 win. Pulford scored twice and Mahovlich potted the winner, his third in six games.

The finals matched two long-time rivals: Toronto vs. Montreal. But the high Imlach forehead was creased in a frown before the final series with Montreal. "The letdown has set in," muttered Punch. "I expected it after the big win over Detroit. My boys are tired and they are not sharp." Indeed, the Leafs appeared to be sluggish in the opener when they were beaten by the Canadiens 4-2. Henri Richard picked up a goal and three assists. Before the game the phenomenal playoff record of the Canadiens was pointed out in a question I put to Toe Blake.

"How many playoff games," I asked him, "have the Habs lost since you took over as coach in 1955-56?"

"Only two, Pete," was Blake's quick reply.

"And how many have you won?"

"All the rest, my friend," he answered, just as quickly.

That meant, that Blake's playoff record, coming into the Leaf series, was 23-2.

Playing a strong defensive game, the Canadiens squeezed out a 2-1 victory in the second game, prompting general manager Frank Selke to state: "This is the greatest hockey team ever assembled."

The Canadiens came up with a 5-2 victory in the third game with Phil Goyette collecting two goals. Henri and Rocket Richard, along with Donnie Marshall, completed the scoring.

When the Rocket scored his goal, he picked me out of the net. It was his

"You hold the cup, Rocket, and I'll wave to your fans. After 82 playoff goals and five straight Stanley Cups, you're the biggest name in hockey . . . ahem . . . next to me, that is."

eighty-second playoff goal and I heard some of his teammates say, "Oh, oh, it looks like the Rocket may be headed for retirement."

Montreal ousted the Leafs 4-0 in the fourth game to make it five Stanley Cups in a row, a remarkable streak. The eight-game playoff sweep equaled the mark set by Detroit in 1951-52.

When all the shouting was over, the Canadiens were very calm about their triumph. Doug Harvey explained why.

"When you win both series, Pete, and win them both in four straight games, there's just not much to get excited about."

Any way you looked at it, the Soviets were "sunk" by Henderson's dramatic goal.

9 Paul Henderson Sinks the Soviets

This is a story about a man who became one of hockey's biggest heroes — a man who won acclaim for a whole country, not just a team or a city—in the early 1970s.

The man's name is Paul Henderson.

Henderson, in the single most dramatic moment in Canada's sporting history, scored the winning goal for Team Canada against the Soviet Union with only thirty-four seconds to play. It's a moment that no hockey fan can ever forget.

What they may have forgotten is that Paul Henderson almost didn't play in the most important game of his life. An injury almost deprived him of his once-in-a-lifetime moment of glory and fame.

Let's go back to a September morning in Moscow. The date was September 28, 1972. The deciding game of the thrilling Team Canada-Russia series would be played in a few hours and there was a chance that one of Canada's stars would be sidelined.

Paul Henderson was not feeling well. He'd fallen heavily into the boards in the previous game, striking his head quite hard. One of the Team Canada doctors, Dr. John Zeldin, examined Henderson and advised him not to play.

"You need a rest, Paul," said Dr. Zeldin. "You took quite a blow. Why not pass up the final game?"

"I can't do that," replied Paul, "unless you tell me I may be risking my life by playing. This may be the most important game of my entire career."

"There *is* a risk if you play," advised the doctor, "but it's probably not a life or death situation. I'd rather you didn't play but the final decision is up to you."

Henderson was fortunate to have a choice. In the previous game he'd been wearing a helmet. Without the helmet, he'd have been badly hurt and probably would have had to watch the final game on television from a hospital bed. Paul was a firm believer in the wisdom of wearing a helmet. While other pros scoffed at the use of helmets, he never took the ice without his firmly in place.

"I've made up my mind," he told the team doctor. "I've decided to play."

Years later, Dr. Zeldin headed up a special clinic for injured athletes in a Toronto hospital. He often discussed the Henderson decision with his patients to demonstrate the fact that sports medicine has special standards.

"Professional athletes often play despite an injury which would sideline the average person," Dr. Zeldin would say. "The pro is trained to carry on despite aches and pains. The pro understands the risks and accepts them. By the same token, an injury that might not bother a pro (like Henderson) could be serious for a young athlete who's still growing."

Now let's get back to Paul and his great moment in Moscow. Ah, but wait. Every big moment needs a buildup. And the buildup to Paul's heroics is a story in itself.

Henderson was advised not to play in what would be the biggest game of his life.

In April, 1972, some Canadian hockey officials returned from Prague, Czechoslovakia with some good news for Canadian fans. The international hockey officials had accepted a Canadian plan for an eight-game series between the Soviet National Team and the best Canadian players from the NHL. Until then, professionals were not welcome in international play.

Hockey has a brief history in the Soviet Union. In 1950, the Central Red Army team won the national title. They wore ill-fitting uniforms and played with little finesse.

Harry Sinden, who had coached the Boston Bruins to a Stanley Cup in 1970, was named manager-coach of the team of Canadian pros. His assistant was John Ferguson, a former Montreal Canadien. The club would be called Team Canada.

Paul Henderson, twenty-nine years old and coming off a big season with the Toronto Maple Leafs, was proud to be selected as a member of what most people called "the strongest hockey club ever assembled."

His hockey travels had taken him from his home town, Lucknow, Ontario to Hamilton, Pittsburgh, Detroit and Toronto. Now he would travel all the way to Moscow to display his skills while millions around the world watched on television.

While Lucknow claimed Paul as a native son, the nearby town of Kincardine was listed in the NHL guide as his birthplace. Some Bruce County residents claim Paul's exact birthplace can never be pinpointed. It was somewhere on the road between Amberley and the hospital in Kincardine, in a sleigh, during a snowstorm, at six o'clock in the morning.

At age eleven, Paul once scored six goals in a peewee tournament game which the Lucknow team won 7-2.

Four years later, in a juvenile game, he scored the staggering total of eighteen goals and set up two others in a 21-3 triumph.

Take it from me, Paul was a fine young hockey player.

When Paul was a young boy growing up, he didn't have an easy life. His diabetic father was an invalid and unable to work. Paul's mother had to raise her children and provide for them herself and often she could barely make ends meet. Paul went to work at fourteen to help out but whenever he had some free time he was down at the local rink playing hockey. He was so good at it, scoring seventy-eight goals in sixteen games one season, that the Detroit Red Wings gave him a try-out with one of their junior teams.

Paul joined the Hamilton Junior Red Wings and became one of their most successful scorers. When he turned pro in 1963, he was expected to be a star right away. Paul, however, needed time to get used to the NHL and it wasn't until he was traded to the Toronto Maple Leafs in 1968 that he finally blossomed. He became a top player for the Leafs and although he was never in the running for the NHL scoring title, he certainly kept the goal judge busy! After scoring thirty-eight goals for the Leafs, Paul was selected to play for Team Canada. No one thought that he would emerge as one of the stars of the series but everyone in hockey knew he could be depended on to do a workmanlike job.

No hockey fan will ever forget Paul's performance in that thrilling series in '72. I know I'll always remember it as one of the most exciting showdowns in the history of the game. There have been other thrilling matchups since, but none can compare with the '72 series. This was the first time Canadian pros had met the champions

In 1950, the Central Red Army club played on artificial ice for the first time in Moscow. It was an outdoor rink measuring a mere forty by forty-two feet.

from the Soviet Union so nobody knew what to expect.

The first four games of the eight game series were played in Canada and things went badly for the Canadians at first. The

Phil Esposito played the finest hockey of his career against the Soviets.

hometown crowds thought Team Canada should have been able to keep zapping me into the Soviet net all night. The Russians, however, had other ideas. In the first game the Soviets came from behind and scored seven goals to Team Canada's three. They shocked a lot of fans who thought Team Canada was unbeatable. After the four games played in Canada, people were even more surprised. The USSR's "amateurs" led the home team two games to one, with one match ending in a tie.

Then it was on to Moscow to finish the series. It was a big change for everyone when we finally arrived in the Soviet Union. The Russians were now the home team and had all the advantages that went with it. The Canadians had become the visitors. They were the ones who had to get used to a whole new system and cope with life on the other side of the Iron Curtain.

We weren't there long when one of the players said to me after an early morning practise, "You know Pete, I don't think I'll ever get used to this place. It's so . . . so different. I mean, I never know what people are talking about and I always feel that every move I make is being watched —whether I'm on or off the ice! The Russians seem to take it for granted but I just can't."

There were a lot of things the Canadians couldn't get accustomed to. One of the main problems was that the Soviets hardly ever let the Canadian players see their wives who had followed the team to Moscow. During meals, the wives ate at one table while the players sat together at the opposite end of the room. When it came to sightseeing, the women went to see things like the Moscow Circus at one time while their husbands had to go at another. About the only time they got to see each other was at night when everyone was exhausted.

Meanwhile the series was attracting incredible interest. The first game in Russia got underway exactly two weeks after the final Canadian game in Vancouver. I don't know if it was the relief of not being the crowd favorite that gave the Team Canada their spark, but they came out flying. In the first two periods they took twenty-five shots and scored three times. I was beginning to wonder what had happened to the Soviets. They seemed to have lost some of their spark. But, by the halfway mark of the third period, I stopped wondering. The Russians turned on the jets and all of a sudden it was the Canadians who looked as if they were standing still. The final score was the Soviet Union 5, Canada 4.

The Soviets now led the series seven points to three. The Canadians faced an almost impossible task—to win overall they had to win the three remaining games. It looked hopeless. But there was one player who wasn't ready to concede anything. And his name was Henderson.

During the first four games in Canada, when the pros were learning just how tough the Russians could be, Paul played well but not spectacularly. It wasn't until that first match in Moscow that he showed everyone what he could do with me. Canada lost the game but Paul had a hand in three of the four goals and it seemed that everytime he got his stick on me, something exciting happened.

It was in the sixth game of the series that Paul really showed his ability for getting the big goals. The Canadians had their backs against the boards. They had to beat the Russians or the series was lost. When they came out on the ice, they looked as if they were ready to take charge but it was the Soviets who scored first on a quick shot to goalie Ken Dryden's left. Team Canada, however, came back and took control. They scored three times in less than two minutes and held on to win 3-2. The goal that proved to be the winner was an unassisted effort by Paul Henderson.

Winning under pressure lifted the Canadians' spirits. As they skated out for the seventh game, I could tell they meant business. They took the lead as they had

Vladislav Tretiak became world famous because of the series. Vlad was sad while Paul was glad when it was over.

Thirty-four seconds to play. Henderson shoots
— and scores!

many times before. The Russians, however, were stubborn and fought back. Play see-sawed back and forth. By the last half of the third period, it was all tied up—but not for long. With just under three minutes left on the clock, Paul Henderson once again gave the Canadians in the crowd something to cheer about. He scored on a pass from Serge Savard and Canada held on to win 4-3.

Now the whole series was riding on the eighth and final game. The two teams were tied, each with three wins and a draw. This was the deciding match. As the players skated out on the ice to begin the final showdown, everyone could feel the tension in the air. It had come down to a matter of pride and both sides wanted to prove their superiority.

The first period was even with neither team outplaying the other. The score after twenty minutes of play was 2-2. In the second period, the Soviets took advantage of every opportunity and led 5-3 after forty minutes. It appeared to be all over for Team Canada and there were a lot of gloomy faces on the Canadian fans in the stands.

But Team Canada rallied in the third. Phil Esposito scored a goal and Yvan Cournoyer got another to tie it at 5-5. Was a tie a fitting way for this remarkable series to end? Some fans said yes, others said no.

I often relive those few moments in Moscow . . . There's less than a minute to play. Henderson grabs me and shoots me into the Soviet zone. He falls down on the play and goes skidding into the boards behind the Soviet net. Three Soviet players have a chance to send me up the ice and out of danger but they all miss me. But Phil Esposito doesn't. He barrels in and takes me on the blade of his stick. I can almost hear him mutter "Come on, Pete, let me take one last shot." Phil whirls around and shoots me at the Soviet goal. In the mean-time, Henderson has scrambled to his feet and is standing right in front of Tretiak. There's nobody near him. Tretiak stops Esposito's shot but the rebound comes right to Henderson. Henderson shoots. Tretiak stops the shot. There's another rebound. Henderson shoots again. He scores!

I'm in the Soviet net and Team Canada wins the game 6-5. Henderson has done it again. He's scored the winning goal with just thirty-four seconds to play. Canada wins the series four games to three with one game tied. The difference in the series is a single goal by Henderson.

Even now, I tingle all over when I think back to that exciting moment in Moscow.

When the Canadians returned home they were met by thirty thousand cheering fans at the Montreal airport. Prime Minister Pierre Trudeau officially welcomed the team back. Montreal Mayor Jean Drapeau, who wanted a victory parade, had ordered three fire engines to the runway. The players rode along the tarmac on the trucks so that the crowd could see their heroes. That final celebration was just one of the things to remember about the 1972 Canada-Russia series. Everybody who played or watched the games will remember different things but I'll bet no one will ever forget Paul Henderson's goal at 19:26 of the third period of the last game.

I'll never forget lying in the goal behind Tretiak. And I know Paul will always remember how he got me there!

"Look, ref! Here comes Unger again. Doesn't the guy ever take a rest?"

10 Unger's Twelve-Year Streak

Every year in the NHL dozens of players spend time riding the bench or sitting in the stands nursing injuries. Even a tough little puck like me gets a few bruises from being slapped into the post once too often. With bone-crunching body checks, fast turns and blistering shots all part of the action, surviving the season without missing at least one game is quite a feat.

There's one fellow, though, who makes it look easy.

Garry Unger, who broke into the NHL in 1967, holds the record of 914 consecutive games played. Not even Gordie Howe has been able to put together that many games. I remember asking Garry one night after a game if the pressure of keeping the streak alive ever bothered him. He just looked me straight in the eye and said, "Pete, playing in the National League has always been my dream and I don't let anything interfere with that. I play every game because I love hockey and I never feel any pressure out there on the ice. I don't think about the record and missing games."

Garry may never have thought about not playing, but that doesn't mean he hasn't come close to sitting out a few times. Perhaps the most serious threat to his streak was an injury he suffered, not in a game but in a riding accident that happened during the off-season. Garry has been a horse lover since he was a youngster and when he had the opportunity he got a ranch of his own. One summer, while he was riding, his horse threw him. In the fall, he broke a bone in his back and was forced to sit out all of training camp. At last, opening night arrived and everyone was wondering, "Will Garry Unger get into the game?"

His fans had nothing to worry about. Not only did Garry play, he even scored a goal on his second shift.

When Garry started out in professional hockey, nobody realized that he was destined to become "Iron Man Unger," holder of the fifth longest consecutive game streak in the history of sports. In 1967-68, when Garry played his first pro game with the Tulsa Oilers of the Central Hockey League, he looked as if he might have potential as a scorer. So he was traded up to Rochester in the American League and finally he joined the Toronto Maple Leafs. He was only with the Leafs for fifteen games when he was traded to Detroit. It was there that people began to notice the blond kid from Edmonton. By the 1969-70 season, Garry was making headlines for both his scoring ability and his off-ice behavior.

Between shooting me into the net forty-two times and being traded to St. Louis, Garry was also dating a reigning Miss America. With his long hair, flashy clothes and expensive cars, Garry looked more like

As a rookie, Garry attracted a lot of attention off the ice. He played in the American Airlines Golf Classic in bare feet while a young lady personally attended to his flowing locks.

a rock star than a hockey star. When he got his skates on, however, no one could deny his talent and he certainly didn't seem to let his private life affect his play on the ice. He always had time for his fans and could often be found at the arena signing autographs and chatting. During his holidays, he liked to get away from the glamor for a while. He spent a lot of time at his ranch with his quarter-horses. Garry simply refused to get caught up in anything that might hurt his game.

Garry's gift for scoring was recognized

Garry played his 914th consecutive game as a
member of the Atlanta Flames.

In a matter of months, Garry was traded from St. Louis to Atlanta to Calgary to Los Angeles.

early in his career but it wasn't until about 1975 that people realized that he was fast closing in on the consecutive games played record. The old mark of 630 was held by a former New York Ranger, Andy Hebenton. By the beginning of 1976, Garry was approaching six hundred games. On March 10th, 1976, Garry finally passed Hebenton's total. After that, everyone started to ask, "How long can he keep going? Will Unger's streak ever end?"

Well, he kept going for another three and a half seasons, but like all streaks, Garry's eventually came to an end. On December 22nd, 1979, Garry Unger finally missed a game. By then he was a member of the Atlanta Flames.

Three games prior to the fateful match, Garry had hurt his shoulder. The injury, however, was not serious enough to prevent him from playing. That night in St. Louis seemed no different. Garry dressed as usual and took his place on the bench. The game went well for the Flames, who were coming off a three-game losing streak. Garry remained on the bench throughout the first and second periods. Everyone assumed that Coach Al MacNeil would use Garry sparingly because of his injury. There were twenty minutes left, easily long enough for Garry to get out on the ice. All he had to do was play one shift and his streak would continue. Time went on, the Flames held a 7-3 lead and Garry still was not sent in. The spectators in the Checkerdome began to ask each other, "When's Garry going to play? There's not much time left."

Even I was starting to wonder where Garry was. With only about three minutes left there was still no sign of him. The crowd was getting restless. Some of the Atlanta players were talking to MacNeil, asking him to let Garry play at least one shift. The coach ignored their pleas. As the last minute of the game ticked away, the fans all started to chant, "Garry, Garry, Garry."

It was no use. Garry Unger stayed on the bench and his streak was over.

Always thinking of his team, Garry said afterwards, "I'm just glad we won, that's what's important. Sure I would've liked to have played but those are the breaks and there's no sense worrying about it. I thought it was really nice of my teammates to try to get me on, but it was up to the coach and I'm sure he just made the decision he thought was in the best interests of the whole team."

Even though Garry Unger's streak is over, he will be long remembered as the player who really earned the name "Iron Man." Garry's streak will always be one of hockey's most talked-about accomplishments and Garry's dedication to the sport will never be forgotten.

He's played almost as many games as I have!

Sawchuk's motto was, "The puck stops here."

11 Sawchuk was a Stingy Guy

When you're a slippery little hockey puck like me, sooner or later you wind up where the players want you to go—in the net. It's not very often I play a full sixty minutes without being "netted" four or five times.

For a goaltender to keep me out of his net for a complete game is quite an accomplishment. It's almost like pitching a no-hitter in baseball. Any goaltender who does so is credited with a shutout.

Whenever somebody mentions the word shutout I always think of the stingiest goalie I ever met—Terry Sawchuk. When I call Sawchuk stingy I mean it as a compliment. He treated a goal like a rare jewel. He hated to give one away.

This kind of attitude, which is quite common among goalies, caused a lot of uncomfortable moments for me and all my rubber relatives. We were bound to be

Peter Puck is in the net. It didn't happen very often when Sawchuk was guarding the goal.

treated rudely if we dared attempt to enter Mr. Sawchuk's cage. It was strictly a case of "no trespassing." He would shoo us away with his big goal stick or catch us in his glove. Once he glared at me and said, "Pete, I've seen just about enough of you. You'd better stay away from here."

I said, "It's not my fault, Terry. I just go where they shoot me. It's all in the game."

While Terry may not have enjoyed my company, I thought he was terrific. He certainly contributed many great moments to hockey. One of his most famous accomplishments took place during the playoffs

in 1952, Terry's second year with the Detroit Red Wings.

By then, Sawchuk had gained something of a reputation as a shutout specialist. I recall the unique style he employed to guard his goal. He crouched low to the ice, so low his huge goal pads seemed to begin right under his chin. I asked him once about his style and he said, "Pete, when I crouch down like that I can see you skimming around the ice a whole lot better."

Anyway, after two big league seasons, Sawchuk had recorded an impressive number of shutouts. Twenty-three of them. But he wasn't thinking about shutouts when the playoffs got underway. He just wanted to help the Red Wings win the Stanley Cup.

Nothing boosts a goalie's confidence like a good start in the Stanley Cup playoffs. Detroit opened against Toronto and Sawchuk was unbeatable. The Leafs fired me in his direction time after time and he calmly turned me aside. Sawchuk's fine play was overshadowed by the parade to the penalty box as the teams established a record for penalty minutes in post-season play. Detroit won 3-0. I had to jump aside to avoid a stream of Red Wing well-wishers when the game was over. Everybody wanted to shake Sawchuk's hand and pound him on the back.

In game two, the Leafs started their veteran netminder Turk Broda against Sawchuk. Broda was thirty-nine years old and overweight and hadn't played in about a year. But he was remarkable that night, allowing only one Red Wing goal. Trouble was, Sawchuk didn't give the Leafs anything. He skated off with a 1-0 victory, his second shutout in a row. The Leafs stood around fuming.

In that game, he made a save that I recall like it was yesterday. The Red Wings picked up a couple of penalties only seconds

In one playoff series, Sawchuk chalked up an astounding goals-against average of 0.62.

apart and Sawchuk was left to defend the goal with only three Detroit defensemen to help him.

Detroit fans groaned when they saw Max Bentley of the Leafs break away with Sid Smith. Both were excellent scorers and Sawchuk braced himself for their assault. Bentley, a nifty stickhandler, pushed me ahead of him confidently. He went right in on goal, made a little deke and passed me smartly over to Smith. But Sawchuk had anticipated the move. Smith's stick rapped me toward the corner. I was certain he would score. Then, Sawchuk's foot shot out and knocked me flying into the boards. What a save! A few seconds later, the Red Wings returned from the penalty box and the Leaf threat was over.

Broda wasn't nearly so sharp in game three and the Wings won their third straight by a 6-2 score. They eliminated the Leafs by a 3-1 score in the fourth game and again, much of the credit went to Sawchuk.

But Sawchuk was just getting warmed up for the final series against the swift Montreal Canadiens.

"Wait'll the kid goalie faces Rocket Richard," crowed one Montreal fan. "We'll see how good he is then."

There was no doubt the Rocket was at his best under Stanley Cup pressure. A year earlier, in the semi-finals, Richard had flattened Detroit's Ted Lindsay with one punch and then scored two big goals in overtime to lead Montreal to an upset victory over the Red Wings.

But this time Sawchuk was ready for the Rocket and his mates. The Detroit net-minder allowed only one goal in the opening game, which the Wings won 3-1.

It was a similar story in game two. One goal for the Canadiens, two for Detroit. Sawchuk's netminding had the Habs talking to themselves. In two languages. Summing up their comments, the ones that could be repeated, it amounted to "My, he's some stingy guy!"

The Canadiens hadn't seen anything yet.

One manager called Terry "the greatest goalie in hockey history."

In the next game Sawchuk didn't allow me near his net. He shut out Montreal. Gordie Howe, then twenty-four years old and having gone scoreless for six previous games, chipped in with a pair of goals in a 3-0 triumph. Ted Lindsay collected the other one and I'll never forget it. He lofted me high in the air and I traveled about sixty-five feet before I skidded crazily into the Montreal net. Lindsay laughed and told me, "Pete, you're my friend for life."

The next game was the big one. Surely Sawchuk was due for an off night. Nobody could remember when they'd seen such goaltending in the playoffs. The Red Wings had won seven straight games, Sawchuk had chalked up three shutouts in two series and the Wings were a threat to become the first team in playoff history to sweep eight straight games on their way to the coveted old cup. The Stanley Cup, that is.

Sawchuk took a deep breath, moved into his familiar crouch and went to work. And

63

what a job he did! Again, he turned aside every Montreal drive. Meanwhile, a fellow named Metro Prystai scored twice for Detroit, Glen Skov scored another and the Red Wings zapped Montreal 3-0.

A fourth shutout for Sawchuk. It was incredible! In eight games, two of hockey's best teams had managed only five goals against him. His goals-against average was almost out of sight, a mere 0.62.

After his Stanley Cup heroics, Frank Boucher, then manager of the New York Rangers, called Sawchuk "the greatest goalie in hockey history. Only two years in the league and already he has twenty-three shutouts. If he keeps it up, he's certain to become the all-time shutout king."

Sawchuk kept it up, all right. Season after season he guarded the Detroit goal, accumulating numerous shutouts. When brilliant young goalie Glenn Hall was pushing Sawchuk for playing time in Detroit, the Red Wings decided to make a move. They traded Sawchuk to Boston where he spent the next couple of seasons.

He became ill in Boston and decided to quit hockey. He was earning $16,000 a year and was the highest paid goalie in pro hockey. But it wasn't enough to keep him in the game. He went back to Detroit to recuperate from mononucleosis.

Six months later, he decided to return to the game but with his old club, the Red Wings. They wanted him back and peddled Glenn Hall to Chicago to make a spot for him. They sent Johnny Bucyk to Boston in the deal for Sawchuk. I always thought it was a deal that worked for both teams.

Sawchuk's second stint with Detroit lasted for seven years and saw him become the all-time leading goaltender for shutouts, topping George Hainsworth's mark of ninety-four.

When he was thirty-four, supposedly all finished, Sawchuk was drafted by Toronto and turned in some fine seasons there. On March 4, 1967, he turned in his hundredth career shutout playing with the Leafs.

When he skated past me after that memorable game, he grinned and said, "That was my centennial project, Pete."

It was Sawchuk's last big season. In the playoffs, he displayed the form of earlier years and paced Toronto to the Stanley Cup.

The next season he was drafted by one of the six new teams joining the league, the Los Angeles Kings. He spent another season back in Detroit as a seldom-used back-up man and his final season was with the New York Rangers.

On February 1, 1970, Sawchuk managed his final shutout. It was number 103, a remarkable total for a career that spanned twenty years.

I really felt sorry when I heard that he died a few months later, following an off-ice accident.

NHL All Time Shutout Leaders

	Years	Games	Shutouts
T. Sawchuk	21	971	103
G. Hainsworth	11	464	94
G. Hall	18	906	84
J. Plante	18	837	82
T. Thompson	12	552	81
A. Connell	12	416	80
*T. Esposito	12	762	79
L. Chabot	11	412	73
H. Lumley	16	803	71
R. Worters	12	488	66
T. Broda	12	628	62
C. Benedict	13	360	58
J. Roach	14	492	58
B. Parent	13	608	55
E. Giacomin	13	610	54
D. Kerr	11	427	51
*R. Vachon	13	688	49
K. Dryden	8	397	46
G. Worsley	21	860	43
C. Gardiner	7	316	42

* Through 1979-80 season

The very first time Bobby took me on his stick,
I knew he was a champion.

12 The Bobby Orr Saga

Of all my friends in hockey over the years, I don't think any can match the achievements of my pal, Bobby Orr.

There have been a lot of heroes since people first started banging me into nets in the early 1900's, but ask someone today who the best player of all time is and chances are they'll say "Number Four, Bobby Orr." Not just the best defenseman—the best *player.* One thing I can say

for sure is that once Bobby grabbed me no one on the other team could touch me. Listen to what some of my other hockey pals say about Robert Gordon Orr:

Brad Park once told me, "When Bobby's on the ice, it's like playing against an extra man." I know what you mean, Brad, and you're no slouch either!

Phil Esposito, who's knocked me into more nets than I can count, called Bobby

Orr "the greatest player in the game. I was happiest when he was on my side!"

Marcel Dionne, who stickhandles so much with me I get dizzy, feels that the "Bobby Orr influence" has found its way into the majority of modern-day young defensemen. "Bobby was the game's biggest star," said Dionne, "and the greatest player. So it was natural that he'd influence young players and how they played the game."

I remember Bobby when he was fourteen and playing top level Junior A hockey with the Oshawa Generals against twenty-year-olds! Even then he smashed all types of records. When he was eighteen he turned professional with the Boston Bruins of the National Hockey League. That was in 1966-67 and Orr went on to win the Calder Trophy as the Rookie of the Year. On top of all that, he was named to the Second All-Star team! Not bad for a rookie, eh?

I'll never forget the night Bobby Orr was "discovered." It was a bantam tournament in a place called Gananoque, Ontario, and two Bruin scouts were there to take a look at a couple of defensemen on the Gananoque team. Before the game was into the second period though, the only player they noticed was a tiny kid wearing Number 2 for Parry Sound—Bobby Orr. The Boston scouts forgot all about the players they had come to see. Shortly after, the Bruins signed Bobby as their property. There was only one problem. Bobby Orr was only fourteen! Needless to say, the Boston team was thrilled to get Orr for themselves.

I don't think any athlete had as much natural talent as Orr did. Oh sure, I know some of my buddies like Barry Basketball and Freddie Football are rolling their eyes and saying, "Oh, there goes Peter again, always bragging about his hockey players." But they were never on Hank Aaron's bat or in Joe Namath's hands as much as I've been on Bobby Orr's hockey stick.

Never has one player controlled and dominated the game like Bobby Orr. His

Bobby won the NHL scoring championship twice — as a defenseman!

tremendous acceleration made his end-to-end dashes a sight to behold. When his knees began giving him trouble, it took away the greatest part of his game—his skating ability. Orr's sense of timing and his hockey sense made him the *smartest* player to ever lace up a pair of skates. He was able to anticipate a play, make one move, and BANG!—I was on his stick once again.

Some say Bobby's talent was something he was born with. Still, Orr worked very hard to develop and make the most of it. Often he made *me* stay late after practise and he'd just shoot, shoot, shoot. He'd come up with moves I'd never seen before.

I think it's funny now—the record for points in a season for a defenseman before Bobby Orr came along was fifty-nine. Bobby not only got 139 points in one season but won the overall scoring title twice! Some defenseman! I remember one jealous NHL defenseman once saying to me that Bobby Orr wasn't a good *defenseman*. I just laughed and reminded him that a defenseman is doing his job if he keeps the opposition from scoring. If someone can do that by scoring himself, so much the better! This player looked at me for a few seconds, and finally said, "You've got a point there, Pete." Then he smashed me down the ice. End of conversation!

Bobby Orr made everyone aware of his extraordinary skills. He virtually owned the right defense position on the year-end All Star team during his playing days. I could go on but I can see I'm making Barry Basketball and Freddie Football a little annoyed.

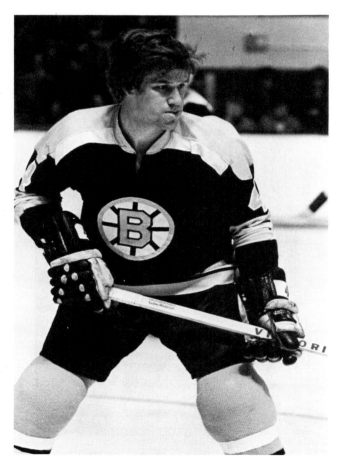

Bobby scored an amazing 264 goals in a ten-year career with the Bruins.

For all of the individual talents Bobby Orr possessed, the one I admired the most was his team play. He could have kept me all to himself, all the time, but instead the team was what mattered to him. What was it he once told me? "I love to score goals and set them up. I don't deny it. But only one thing will make this season a success and that's if our team gets the Stanley Cup. Nothing else matters." Right you are, Bobby!

Bobby gave back as much as he took from hockey. You could find him visiting sick children in hospitals, signing endless autographs, trying to answer every piece of mail, or speaking as the honorary chairman for the March of Dimes or the Muscular Dystrophy Association. It was a huge loss to all sport when Bobby's knees could no longer stand the constant punishment and pain and he was forced to retire at the age of thirty. In his over ten years of NHL play, Bobby managed to complete the entire schedule only once.

The NHL didn't completely lose the services of Bobby Orr though. In late 1979, Orr was hired by the league to be NHL president John Ziegler's special assistant. I always knew that once Bobby decided to stop knocking me around he'd remain in hockey in some way. The National Hockey League is the big winner. I wish him all the luck in the world.

Now let me tell you about one of Bobby's biggest nights—Bobby Orr Night at the Boston Garden. Most of my greatest moments in hockey were the result of some rare performances of individual skill on ice—like Darryl Sittler's ten point night or Terry Sawchuk's shutout wizardry. Just as many thrills were produced by inspired team efforts—like the Philadelphia Flyers undefeated streak during the 1979-80 season and the U.S. Olympic Team's fabulous triumph at Lake Placid.

But there's one night that stands out in my memory, a night that made even my hard rubber body all but melt with emo-

My hard rubber body all but melted with emotion on Bobby Orr Night, especially when he put on his Number 4 jersey.

tion. Oddly enough, no star player smashed me into the net a startling number of times that night. No team celebrated a hard-fought final series by sipping champagne from the Stanley Cup. In fact, this memorable moment took place on the ice at the Boston Garden on January 9, 1979. The whole thing only lasted thirty minutes and during that time no goals were scored, no penalties called and no records established.

It was Bobby Orr Night at the Boston Garden.

What a tribute Bobby received from the sellout crowd! They poured out their affection to the man who ruled the ice lanes at the Boston Garden for a decade, a man who changed the whole pattern of hockey, a man who boldly played his position like no one had ever played it before.

"It was tougher to get a ticket for this game than any game in Bruin history, including Stanley Cup games," marveled the Bruins' public-relations man Nate Greenberg. "You're lucky, Pete. You get in free."

When Bobby appeared, head down, wearing a new pin-stripe suit, the crowd stood and screamed their welcome.

"Baw-bee, Baw-bee, Baw-bee."

Don Cherry, who was coaching Boston that year, picked me up and sat me down on top of the boards by the Boston bench so that I could get a good view of the ceremony.

Over the din he shouted, "There'll never be another like him, Pete."

"Baw-bee, Baw-bee, Baw-bee."

With his wife by his side, Bobby grinned and waved at the fans who jammed every corner of the old arena.

Five, seven, ten minutes. The cheering went on and on.

While the ovation continued, it left time to reflect on the career of this player the fans came to honor.

He scored an amazing 264 goals and assisted on 624 others in a brilliant ten-year career as a Bruin. He won the Norris

When Bobby appeared, wearing a new pin-stripe suit, the crowd stood and screamed their welcome.

Trophy as best defenseman eight times, the Hart Trophy as most valuable player three times and the Ross Trophy as NHL scoring champion twice. For a defenseman to win the scoring title was unheard of—a feat unparalleled in the history of hockey. For six straight years he finished with more than a hundred points. One season he scored forty-six goals from his defense position and added eighty-nine assists to lead the scoring parade with 135 points. Until Bobby came along, only one defenseman, a player named Flash Hollett, had ever scored twenty goals in a season. Bobby broke Hollett's record in his second season, scoring his twenty-first goal on his twenty-first birthday.

No Boston fan will ever forget the fourth game of the Stanley Cup final in 1970 and the sudden-death overtime against the St.

In 1976, Bobby finally played against the Soviets and was named Most Valuable Player of the Canada Cup Series.

Louis Blues. Orr took a pass from Derek Sanderson and fired the puck into the St. Louis net just as he was tripped. He flew through the air like an eagle and when he skidded to the ice, he knew his shot had won the Stanley Cup, ending twenty-nine years of playoff frustration for Boston.

There was the Canada Cup competition in 1976. Bobby's bad knees had kept him out of the historic Russia-Canada matches in 1972 but he was determined to play in the Canada Cup. If his legs bothered him, he never let on, and for the duration of the Canada Cup matches he performed brilliantly. After Team Canada won the championship game with Czechoslovakia, Bobby was named Most Valuable Player.

Shortly after, his aching knees failed him and he sat out the 1977-78 season, hoping a long rest would help. It didn't. By then, the Bruins had allowed him to escape to Chicago, which wasn't very smart. Bobby should never have worn any uniform but the Bruins.

He tried to come back as a Black Hawk but the underpinning was loose and unreliable. So on Nov. 8, 1978, a few days after he scored his final NHL goal (his 270th) against Rogie Vachon of Detroit, he announced his retirement as a player at a news conference in Chicago.

Orr fought back the tears as he said, "I had to try just once more to make it back. I owed it to myself. But I'm not able to play or practise properly and I don't want to stand in the way of others who can contribute more."

Six knee operations ended Orr's career.

I've often thought it sad that none of us will ever know how great he might have been. He skated on bad knees ever since he was a junior star in Oshawa, Ontario. A healthy Orr, playing for two decades instead of one, might have set standards that would last for a lifetime. Even the records he did establish provide a difficult challenge for today's superstars and those who will rise to the fore in years to come.

Coach Don Cherry and his famous dog Blue. We watched from rinkside the night Bobby was honored.

Two other record-setters, Bobby Hull and Gordie Howe, have been lavish in their praise for Orr since he entered the league as a crewcut teenager in 1966.

"He's absolutely the greatest player I've seen come into the league since I've been around," said Hull.

"Oh, Bobby must have some flaws in his game somewhere," drawled Howe. "The trouble is, so far I haven't been able to find any of them."

Johnny Bucyk, a former Bruins' captain and one of Bobby's teammates for most of his career, moved to center ice to join Bobby and his wife Peggy. Bucyk unfolded a Bruin sweater with Bobby's famous Number 4 on the back. Bobby held it aloft and then placed it over his arm. The crowd responded.

"Put it on. Put it on."

Bobby laughed and took off his suitcoat. He pulled the sweater over his head. There was a great roar of approval.

Then, right over center ice, they raised a large banner. Bobby's name and number were on the banner and the years spanning his career as a Bruin—1966-76.

Bobby's thank you speech was brief and difficult to hear over the roar of the crowd. It produced another three-minute ovation.

He then shook hands with all of the Bruins and with Massachussets Senator Edward Kennedy who was in a seat behind the Boston bench.

As he left the arena, Bobby saw me and waved.

"I'm going to miss you, Pete. We had some good times together, didn't we?"

"We sure did, Bobby," I replied with a quivering voice. "Good luck and God bless you."

Then the tears filled my eyes.

I learned later that Orr consented to the day in his honor only if any money raised went to charity. As a result, more than $18,000 was divided among his four favorite causes—multiple sclerosis, cystic fibrosis, the Boston Children's Hospital and a private fund for research into a rare brain disease which took the life of a daughter of one of Bobby's close friends.

Robert Crane, another good friend of Bobby's and the state treasurer, said, "People have no idea how many hundreds of hours he has devoted to charity in the city of Boston and how many times he visited hospitals. Bobby would get angry if there was ever any publicity about the things he did. The people here loved him as a great athlete and the definitive team player. But their love goes much beyond that. He's a very special person in our hearts."

A Boston priest, Rev. Frank Chase, once said of Orr. "The world is full of little people—like myself. We need our heroes and our superstars to whom we can look for inspiration. It is not easy to be a superstar—to remember the good that an autograph or a handshake can do. Bobby Orr does those things all the time."

Don Cherry has often referred to the Boston fans as "the toughest crowd in the world."

But on Bobby Orr Night they were the softest.

"All goalies owe you a vote of thanks, Jacques. By insisting on wearing the face mask, you revolutionized the art of puckstopping and made the game safer."

13 The Masked Marvel

One of my all-time favorite goalies is Jacques Plante. What a marvel he was in goal, a real Peter Puck stopper. I was in Philadelphia recently and I bumped into Jacques at the Spectrum. He was busy coaching some young goalies.

"Hi, Jacques. It's me, Peter Puck."

"Hello, Pete. It's good to see you again."

"Is it really, Jacques? I'll bet you wouldn't say that if you were still playing goal in the NHL."

"You're right, Pete," Jacques chuckled. "When I was a player I never wanted to see you. The farther you stayed away from me the better I liked it. You're the little guy who kept spoiling my goals-against average."

"That wasn't all my fault, Jacques. Blame guys like Gordie Howe and Bobby Hull. They're the guys who zapped me into your net all those times. But you always stopped a lot more shots than you let in.

The hockey masks of today are colorful.

Hockey fans will never forget you, Jacques. Why, you were one of the greatest goalies ever to play the game."

"Thanks, Pete. I always enjoyed playing goal. Every game, every shot was a challenge and I always worked hard to improve my game. I was very proud to be a player in the NHL."

Jacques waved goodbye and went off to coach his young goaltenders. I sat at rinkside and watched him offer tips and advice. He could talk about goaltending for hours. It was true he'd revolutionized the art of puckstopping. It was also true he might have been the first goalie killed in the course of a hockey game.

I shuddered to think of the night he came so close to death, only to be saved by his mask. Ah, the face mask, the controversial face mask. Once scoffed at by hockey men (few of them were goalies) and said to be a handicap, not a help, the face mask fought a long, hard fight to gain hockey respectability.

Once considered to be as useful as a broken stick, the face mask is now a vital piece of equipment in every goaltender's bag. Hundreds of goalies have been saved from thousands of stitches by wearing a face mask, and some, like Plante, have been saved from crippling injuries and possibly even death through its use.

Because Jacques Plante was just as stubborn off the ice as he was between the goalposts, the face mask became a popular item in pro hockey. Not as popular as Peter Puck, perhaps, but pretty close. Who made it popular? Why, Jacques Plante did. I'll never forget the night he wore it for the first time in the NHL. The date was November 1, 1959, a memorable moment for all goaltenders.

Goalie Gilles Gratton introduced this toothy mask, designed to frighten opposing forwards.

With Plante defending the goal, the Montreal
Canadiens won one Stanley Cup after another.

Jacques Plante was at his acrobatic best
that November night at Madison Square
Garden. The Montreal Canadiens were on
their way to a record five straight Stanley
Cup victories and Plante was hockey's pre-
mier goaltender.

I was slapped around particularly hard
that night. The Rangers' Andy Bathgate
had developed a powerful slapshot over the
years and when he trapped me on his stick,
then brought his arms and shoulders into
his shot, I braced myself. I knew I was in
for a ride like a rocket.

Midway through the game, Bathgate
grabbed me. "Here you go, Pete," he yelled
as he slapped me through a crowd of
players gathered in front of Plante.

"Look out, Jacques," I screamed as I
rocketed toward the Montreal goal.

It was too late. Jacques couldn't see me
and I crashed into his face. He fell down,

bleeding from the nose and cheek. His
teammates gathered around and the Montreal trainer came out on the ice. They
helped Jacques to his feet and assisted him
to the dressing room.

A doctor came in and stopped the bleeding. Then he carefully placed seven stitches
in the wound.

In those days, big league teams carried
just one goalie. If a goalie was badly
injured, a substitute (often a rank amateur) usually was called upon to play the
position. In New York, the sub was Joe
Schaefer, a little-known netminder without
Plante's talent.

Montreal coach Toe Blake said to
Jacques, "Can you go back out there?"

"I can and I will," said Jacques, "But I
won't go back on the ice without my face
mask."

Blake looked at him and nodded. He

knew he must let Plante have his way.

Plante had been experimenting with an odd-looking mask for several months. He'd used it in practice but never in a game.

When he first donned the mask, some players and coaches suggested that he'd lost his courage.

Plante just laughed.

"You wouldn't jump out of a plane without a parachute, would you?" he asked. "That would be stupid in my book, not courageous. I have just as much courage with the mask on or off. But I'm better with it on."

That night in New York he wiped the blood off his face and put on the mask.

He returned to the ice and a curious hush fell over the crowd.

"Hey, funny face," yelled a fan. "Who you hiding from?"

"Halloween was last month," sneered another.

Plante ignored the jibes and took his place in goal. He knew he must perform well if he hoped to silence critics of the mask. He stopped everything the Rangers threw at him. The only goal the Rangers scored came on a rebound. Montreal won the game and the Habs' winning streak went to eight games.

They won the next game and the game after that. With Plante performing brilliantly, Montreal's unbeaten streak reached eighteen games. Plante and his face mask were the talk of the league.

When the Canadiens slumped late in the season, Coach Blake suggested the mask might be partially to blame. "It may be affecting Plante's play," he suggested. "Perhaps he should try playing without it and see what happens."

Plante agreed to put the mask aside for the next game. The Canadiens were promptly beaten by Detroit 3-0.

"That's it," stated Plante. "I'll never play without the mask again."

Jacques Plante enjoyed many fine seasons in Montreal. Then, suddenly, in a

Plante chases his goal stick. Early in his career, he startled everybody by skating well out of his goal.

blockbuster deal, he was traded to the New York Rangers. After two seasons in New York, Jacques called it quits. He moved back to Montreal and spent his time writing a sports column for a newspaper and playing in oldtimers' games.

Then, when the NHL expanded to double its size in 1967, there was a need for experienced goaltenders. The two-goalie system was introduced and salaries were

At age 47, Plante was still playing in the WHA.

series against Boston, the Blues and the Bruins were tied 1-1 in the second period. The Bruins got a power play and the puck moved swiftly into the St. Louis defensive zone. Boston's Fred Stanfield took a sizzling slapshot from inside the blue line. He zapped me toward Plante. I'm sure Jacques would have stopped me with his glove or deflected me with his stick but then, at the last instant, Phil Esposito's stick got in the way. I was tipped upward by Phil's stick and thudded into Plante's mask. I've never hit a goalie any harder and you could hear the crack from the impact all over the arena. Jacques was carried off and later he said, "I remember Stanfield shooting and that's all. Then I felt the pain . . . such pain. I didn't know where I was. But inside me I knew one thing . . . the face mask had saved my life."

That was the last game Plante ever played for St. Louis. He was sold to Toronto before the next season. After almost three seasons in a Leaf uniform he moved on to Boston.

Then he accepted a new challenge as general manager of the Quebec Nordiques of the WHA. When the Nordiques struggled to a fifth place finish he resigned and went back to tending goal.

His final season was in the WHA with Edmonton, a forty-seven-year-old wonder whose lengthy career spawned several hundred great moments.

But the moment I remember, the one all goalies should thank him for, was that night in New York when he put the mask on and refused to take it off.

skyrocketing. When Jacques was drafted by Scotty Bowman's St. Louis Blues he jumped at the chance to get back into hockey.

A second great moment in his career took place while he was performing for the Blues. With Plante and another oldtimer, Glenn Hall, sharing the goaltending duties, the Blues reached the Stanley Cup finals for three straight years.

In the opening game of the 1970 final

Brrr . . . it gets cold in the Yukon.

14 Dawson City Daredevils

In the last few years I've heard a lot of people around the NHL talking about how difficult it is for the teams on the west coast to go east. Whenever someone mentions the problem of getting from one game to another, I always think about the team that must still hold the record for long-distance traveling.

Back in 1904, a team from Dawson City in the Yukon issued a challenge to the most successful team of the decade, the Ottawa Silver Seven. The Dawson City Daredevils, as they were nicknamed, wanted to play the Silver Seven for the Stanley Cup. Now, back then, there was no regular season or organized playoffs and any team could challenge for Lord Stanley's trophy. As long as the defending champs accepted, the two sides played a short series for the cup.

But the games almost didn't get played.

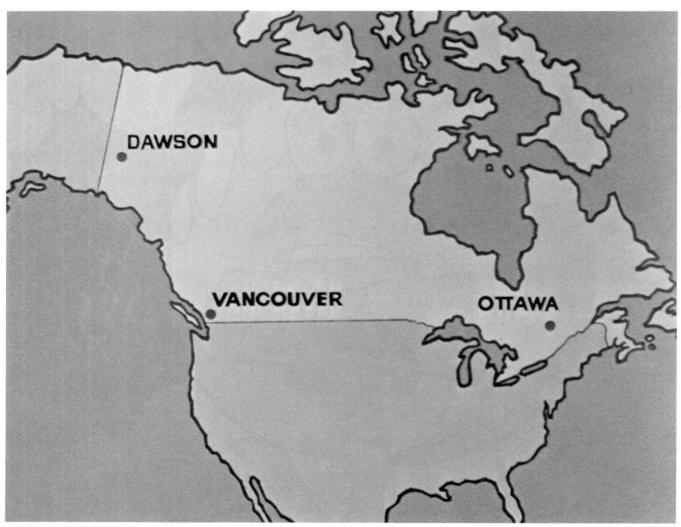

On December 19, 1904, the Dawson City players set out for Ottawa — by dogsled!

The Ottawa Silver Seven had outscored and outfought all the best teams in Ontario and Quebec. They laughed at the idea of playing some third-rate team nobody had ever heard of.

"After all", they said, "What would anyone from the Yukon know about hockey?" At last, though, they decided to go along with the joke and play the team from the Klondike. The only problem now was how were the Daredevils going to get from Dawson City to Ottawa? Seventy-five years ago there were no airplanes or even any team buses. But the team from Dawson was determined to bring home the Stanley Cup. They weren't going to let something like a few thousand miles stand in the way. They persuaded a wealthy prospector, Colonel Joe Boyle, to put up the cash for the journey. On December 19th, 1904, the Daredevils set out . . . by dogsled! The whole town was there to see them off and it must have been quite something. They were heading for the Alaska coast where they were going to make connections with a ship to Seattle. From Seattle, they planned to take a train north to Vancouver, then east across the Rockies and on to Ontario.

Unfortunately, they forgot to make allowances for the weather. I know how cold

I get in the freezer before a game but it's not nearly as bad as an Arctic winter. The Daredevils had to make their way in bitter cold, with the temperature below −20°F and chilling winds. They also suffered from blistered feet and exhaustion on the long dogsled drive to Skagway, Alaska. When at last they reached their destination, they immediately headed for the harbor, but they were too late. They'd missed the boat to Seattle by only two hours!

The next boat didn't come into port until five days later but those fellows from Dawson City didn't give up. Some of the townspeople took them in and gave them a chance to rest for a while. When the boat arrived the Daredevils were ready to go. The trip down the coast was rough but everyone was so eager to get to Ottawa that they hardly noticed. In Seattle they boarded a Vancouver-bound train and began another leg of their journey.

It wasn't until they were well east of the Rockies that they discovered they were famous throughout Canada. Wherever the train stopped, hockey fans poured onto the platform to wish the team from the Klondike luck against the mighty Silver Seven. It was amazing how popular the Daredevils were, considering that no one had every heard of them before. Those eight men quickly became household names. They had come from all over the country and had been brought together by their love of hockey. The youngest team member was seventeen years old—Albert Forrest, the goalie who came from Three Rivers. The defensemen were Jim Johnstone from Ottawa and Dr. Randy McLennon from Cornwall. On the forward line were left winger George Kennedy, center Hec Smith and rover Dave Fairbairn, all from Manitoba, and right winger Norm Watt from Aylmer.

This was the rink in Dawson City in 1900. Some of these players may have been on the team that challenged Ottawa in 1905.

There was also an extra man, A.N. Martin, from Ottawa.

At last they reached Ottawa. The date was January 12, 1905. It had taken them nearly a month to travel four thousand miles. They were all exhausted from their trek but the Silver Seven refused to postpone the games and let the Daredevils get some practise.

When the two teams finally took to the ice, the team from Dawson City looked as if they'd forgotten how to skate. The game quickly got underway and the puck was soon whizzing all over the ice with at least one member of the Silver Seven never far away. The Daredevils hadn't got their ice legs back yet and were having a tough time keeping up with the swift-skating Ottawa team. Poor Albert Forrest had to stop so many shots that he lost track. The Dawson City team, however, didn't give up. They showed the determination that had brought them to Ottawa and as they got

the feel of the ice under their skates again they began to fight back. But they were unable to overcome the Silver Sevens' huge lead and in the end they were outscored 9-2.

Despite the fact that they took such a drubbing, the Daredevils had accomplished something really surprising. They had managed to hold Ottawa's most dangerous shooter, Frank McGee, to only one goal. After the match all the Dawson City players gathered in an Ottawa tavern to talk over the game. One of the local fans brought up the name of McGee. A Dawson City forward remarked, "For such a great player he sure didn't do anything spectacular. We thought he'd be something special, but he's not so hot after all!"

The tavern fell silent. Nobody ever talked about Frank McGee like that. Then the Ottawa supporter who had first mentioned McGee laughed and said, "This guy doesn't think Frank's so great, everybody. Maybe I

One-eyed Frank McGee set many records in the two-game series.

The Dawson City goalie should have boarded up the net. It was the only way to stop McGee.

should tell Frank that he ain't makin' a very good impression on the visitors. Maybe then he'll really show 'em what he can do."

He must have made good on his threat to tell Frank what those upstarts were saying about him, because in the second game, Frank McGee set records that have never been equaled. In the first half, he scored four goals right at the start but it wasn't till the second that he really got down to work. He scored ten times including eight consecutive goals, three of which were in a span of ninety seconds. The final score was 23-2. I always thought that I had been zapped by the best shooters in the world but just thinking about Frank McGee makes my head spin!

Even though they came away empty-handed, things were not all bad for the team from the Yukon. They had captured the imagination of the fans with their daring challenge for the Stanley Cup and were responsible for the first sell-out match in hockey's history. They had also provided the game with some of its most memorable moments. Those Daredevils from Dawson City will always be remembered for their grim determination, if not their skill.

The Rocket once scored fifty goals in fifty games. No wonder Montreal fans loved him.

15 Some Big Little Moments

It's easy to remember the greatest moments in my long hockey career, the amazing individual performances and the thrilling team efforts that resulted in Stanley Cup triumphs.

But along the way, there have been dozens of other moments that I recall with delight. Some were exciting, some were amusing and some were unusual.

I call them Peter Puck's big little moments.

The Night the Rocket Won All Three Stars

It happened in 1944 after a Stanley Cup playoff game at the Montreal Forum. Rocket Richard, only twenty-three years old, scored all five goals in Montreal's 5-1 rout of Toronto. After all games at the Forum, the game's three stars traditionally skate out and take a bow. On this night, the standing room crowd was able to give a continuous ovation to the hero of the game. Star number one was—Rocket Richard. Star number two was—Rocket Richard. And star number three was—Rocket Richard.

The Man Who Tried to Steal the Stanley Cup

At the Chicago Stadium in 1962, an avid Montreal fan was suffering through a playoff game between the Canadiens and the Black Hawks. The Hawks were well in front and appeared certain to win the Cup. The fan could stand it no longer. In the third period he left his seat, walked into the stadium lobby and stood in front of a large glass showcase housing the famous Stanley Cup. Suddenly, he reached out and jimmied open the case, threw the cup over his shoulder and marched out of the stadium. Two ushers took off in pursuit, caught the culprit and struggled with him until police arrived.

The fan's explanation: "I was just taking the cup back to Montreal. That's where it rightfully belongs."

Which goes to show—there's no easy way to get the cup.

"Your honor, I wasn't *stealing* the cup. I was just taking it back to Montreal where it belongs."

Rags to Riches

Not so long ago Charlie Simmer was riding the buses in the minor leagues. Then, midway through the season, he was called up to the Los Angeles Kings. Nobody counted on Simmer to provide Kings' fans with many exciting moments during the 1979-80 season, even though he'd finished the previous season by scoring goals in five straight games for the Kings.

But when the 1979-80 season got underway, Simmer promptly potted goals in six straight games. That came to a total of eleven straight goal-scoring games and surpassed the NHL record of ten straight shared by Andy Bathgate and Mike Bossy. But they were stars. Simmer wasn't.

The NHL refused to recognize Simmer's streak because it spanned two seasons. There was only one thing to do—start another streak. Simmer banged in goals from far out and close in. He scored on breakaways, rebounds and tip-ins. And he didn't stop until he'd scored in thirteen straight games—an all-time record.

Now everybody knows Charlie Simmer and everybody is happy that he too has become a star. Except perhaps the goalies.

The Curse of Muldoon

When Pete Muldoon, coach of the Chicago Black Hawks, was fired after the 1926-27 season, legend has it that he placed a curse on the Hawks, predicting: "This team will never finish first." Most hockey men believe the famous "curse" was the figment of a sportswriter's imagination. Still, the Hawks played for forty-one years before finishing at the top of the league standings.

The Battle of the Bulge

In 1949, Toronto got off to a bad start, and Conn Smythe felt that his goalie, Turk Broda, was overweight. He ordered him to lose seven of his 197 pounds and set a

Conn Smythe ordered Turk Broda to lose weight in hockey's "Battle of the Bulge."

deadline, snapping "We're not running a fat man's club." To make his point even stronger, he engineered a trade the next day for Al Rollins, a lanky goaltender, *and* he recalled little Gil Mayer from Pittsburgh. Mayer, ironically, was on a diet too—trying to *gain* weight.

Broda's battle with a bulging waistline made great news copy. He made the weight with eight ounces to spare and returned to regular duty.

The Youngest Referee

Ages of early-day referees in Stanley Cup play were seldom recorded but Frank Patrick would certainly rank among the youngest. Frank was not only a star player but he refereed in the Montreal Senior League at age eighteen and handled a Stanley Cup game at age twenty.

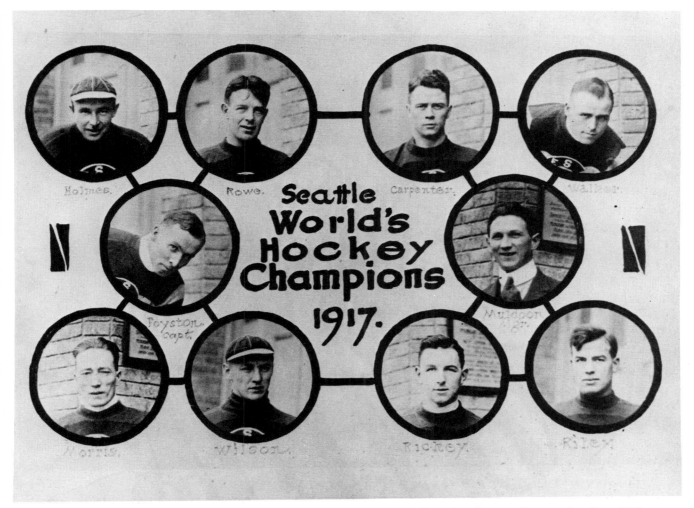

The Seattle Metropolitans, the first U.S. team to win the Stanley Cup.

The First American Team to Win the Stanley Cup

In 1916-17, the year before the birth of the NHL, the Seattle Metropolitans won the Stanley Cup. Seattle beat the Montreal Canadiens three games to one. Bernie Morris was Seattle's biggest star with fourteen goals in the series, six in one game.

Bill Durnan's Shutout Streak in 1948

Bill Durnan, who had to be coaxed into playing another season with Montreal Canadiens after the home fans jeered him in 1947-48, set a modern record for NHL goaltending on March 9 in Chicago.

Durnan had a string of four straight shutouts and 283 minutes and 45 seconds of scoreless play going into the Hawk-Canadien game. He held the Hawks scoreless in the first period, but his streak ended at 5:36 of the second period when Gaye Stewart scored. That gave him 309:21 without a goal being scored against him, surpassing the 290:12 mark set by the Hawks' Charlie Gardiner in 1930.

The Night Bernie Parent Lost his Face Mask

In a playoff game in 1972 between New York and Toronto, the teams began fighting. Parent, then the Leaf goalie, had his

I'm with you, ref. That was a tough decision
but a fair one.

mask snatched away by a Ranger player
who threw it into the stands. The mask was
not returned and Jacques Plante had to
finish the game for Parent.

A few days later, Parent's mask was sent
back to him by mail to Toronto. It arrived
in a plain brown box. There was no letter of
explanation.

This Coach Was Angry!

Tommy Gorman, who coached the Black
Hawks to a Stanley Cup in 1934, once
became so incensed over a ruling by referee

Bill Stewart that he pulled his players off
the ice. Stewart gave Gorman one minute
to get them back on again. When Gorman
refused, Stewart dropped the puck at center ice. Cooney Weiland of Boston skated in
and fired the puck into the empty net to
snap a 2-2 tie. It was the only time a game
was forfeited and it went into the books as
a Boston victory.

The Moment Mikita Grew Up

Stan Mikita, possibly the greatest player
ever to wear a Chicago Black Hawk uni-

form, retired at the end of the 1979-80 season. His uniform Number 21 became the first Black Hawk jersey to be retired.

Stan scored 541 career goals. He captured four Art Ross Trophies as the NHL's leading scorer; two Hart Trophies as Most Valuable Player and two Lady Byng Trophies for sportsmanship.

Winning his first Lady Byng Trophy was one of the most satisfying moments in Mikita's distinguished career. In 1964-65 the clever Hawk centerman spent 154 minutes in the penalty box. He was a chippy player, mean with the stick and quick with the elbows.

Then he made a remarkable transformation. He changed his style and cleaned up his act. His penalty minutes shriveled to twelve minutes and he was rewarded with the Lady Byng.

Asked to explain the turn around, Stan said, "I just grew up, that's all. Plus the fact I discovered I couldn't fight. Oh, yes, there's one other reason. My little daughter said to me 'Daddy, why are you always sitting all alone on that little bench when all the other players are sitting together?' That kind of got through to me."

The Only Year the NHL Failed to Declare a Champion

In 1919 Montreal Canadiens traveled to Washington to meet the Seattle Metropolitans, champions of the Pacific Coast Hockey Association in the Stanley Cup final series.

There was an influenza epidemic throughout North America. Bad Joe Hall of the Canadiens was hospitalized by flu on his arrival in Seattle. Then more members of the Canadiens' team became ill and the Seattle department of health canceled the series. Hall died a few days later and George Kennedy, the Canadiens' manager, died from the effects of the virus two years later.

Frank Patrick, president of the PCHA,

Frank (King) Clancy played every position, including goal, in a Stanley Cup playoff game. Clancy is now an executive with the Toronto Maple Leafs.

did not wish to accept the cup by default. No Stanley Cup champions were named that year.

The Player Who Played Every Position in a Playoff Game

Frank (King) Clancy, who was with Ottawa Senators in the 1923 playoffs, played all three forward and two defensive positions in a series against Vancouver.

Then he even got a chance to play goal. Ottawa goalie Clint Benedict was given a two-minute penalty. In those days the goaltender served his time like the other players.

Benedict tossed his stick to Clancy, saying, "Take care of that net 'til I get back." Clancy was not scored on and Ottawa went on to win the series and the Stanley Cup.

It's appropriate for me to end this book with a story about Mr. Clancy. He has always been one of my favorite hockey men. Mr. Clancy's motto is the same as mine—"if you don't have fun, what's the sense of playing?"

So have fun, guys and girls, and remember: Love that hockey game!

I hope you enjoyed reading about many of hockey's biggest moments. It was a thrill for me to be a part of them.

If you like to read fiction as well as fact, look for my new book *Peter Puck and the Stolen Stanley Cup.* It's all about a thief who runs off with the game's most prized trophy and guess who tracks him down? That's right, the imp of the ice. Pretty soon, they'll be calling me Detective Peter Puck.

Next time they put me in the freezer I'm going to begin my third hockey book. It's cold in the freezer but it's quiet there and I can concentrate. Besides, with two books behind me, I might as well go after the old hat trick.

Best of luck from your rubbery writer, your, ahem, Shakespeare of shinny, and above all your friend,

Peter Puck

LOVE THAT HOCKEY GAME!